Body of Work

Also by Maggie O'Sullivan

In the House of the Shaman (1993)
Red Shifts (2001)
Palace of Reptiles (2003)
"all origins are lonely" (2003)

(with Bruce Andrews)
eXcLa (1993)

As editor:
Out of Everywhere: linguistically innovative poetry
by women in North America and the UK (1996)

Audio:
her/story:eye (CD, 2004)
States of Emergency (CD, 2005)

Maggie O'Sullivan
BODY OF WORK

REALITY STREET
2006

Published by
Reality Street Editions
63 All Saints Street, Hastings, East Sussex TN34 3BN
www.realitystreet.co.uk

Copyright © Maggie O'Sullivan, 2006
Cover painting: *Icened Mollusc*, by Antony Cook (oil & acrylic on canvas,
1x2 metres), 1987
Typesetting & book design by Ken Edwards

Printed and bound in Great Britain by CPI Antony Rowe, Eastbourne

A catalogue record for this book is available from the British Library

ISBN-10: 1-874400-36-9
ISBN-13: 978-1-874400-36-3

For Antony Cook
(25 February 1936 – 1 April 2005)

Contents

Acknowledgements

Body of Work brings together the nine booklets of London-based work made between 1975 and 1987 and presents the works in the order in which they were actually created. It reprints seven out-of-print booklets (1982-88) – acknowledgement to the publishers is made below – and prints for the first time in book form, the previously unpublished *tonetreks* (1978) and *POINT.BLANK.RANGE* (1984). Although originally planned as booklets, it was an accident of fate that these two works remained unpublished until now.

tonetreks (made between 1975 and 1977) previously unpublished in book form
Front/back cover images by Antony Cook (1978)

Concerning Spheres (Bristol: Broken Ground Press, 1982)

Un-Assuming Personas (London: Writers Forum, 1985)
first published in *Reality Studios*, Volume 4, 1982

A Natural History in 3 Incomplete Parts (London: Magenta, 1985)
Part 1 published as *An Incomplete Natural History*, Writers Forum, 1984

From the Handbook of That & Furriery (London: Writers Forum, 1986)

Divisions of Labour (Newcastle-Upon-Tyne: Galloping Dog, 1986)

POINT.BLANK.RANGE (made 1984) previously unpublished in book form
pages 1 and 2 published as front/back covers for *Divisions of Labour*
pages 9-16 incl. published in *Reality Studios*, Volume 6, Interface issue, 1984

States of Emergency (Oxford: ICPA, 1987)
excerpts published in *Angel Exhaust* and *Writing*

Unofficial Word (Newcastle-Upon-Tyne: Galloping Dog, 1988)
excerpts published in *Raddle Moon 5*

Foreword: Maggie O'Sullivan's Medleyed Verse

Every poem was once a word.

If culture were an accident, then the job of the poet might be to write the report rather than rectify the wrong. If culture were the product of a supreme fiction, then the poet's job might be to find the authors and clue them into things – not as they are but as they appear.

Maggie O'Sullivan is the poet of the "unofficial" word. In this sense, and perhaps paradoxically, O'Sullivan is in a main line of British poets, a line that swerves, with clinamacaronic speed, from Blake to Swinburne, MacDiarmid to Raworth, Carroll to Bergvall, Cowper to Loy, Kwesi Johnson to Bunting, Rossetti to Fisher. In their own way, each of these is an anti-representative poet: one who takes the office of poetry as the creation of spaces between sanctions; outside, that is, received categories.

You can't make a poem unless you are willing to break some verses.

In *Roots of Lyric: Primitive Poetry and Modern Poetics*, Andrew Welsh makes the distinction between "song melos" (with its externally derived regular meter) and "charm melos" (whose more chaotic sound patterns emerge internally). O'Sullivan's poetry is unmistakably *charm*. In a key work of poetics, "river-running (realizations" (in *Palace of Reptiles*), she put it this way: "A Song Said Otherwise, half sung / half said SINGS"; where "Otherwise" is also a music that is "Edgewise," wise to edges and others and also edgy; othering and auditing rather than authoring.

To half-sing a song is to stutter into poetry and back to music, your back to the music, part incantation, part pleat. "Stammering before speech", O'Sullivan writes in "riverrunning (realizations": not just *prior to* but *in the face of*. The beat is off mark so as to be on tangent. A stone thrown into a pond (pound, pun) produces rings of concentric circles around the point of entry. The charm is to create a rhythm in the counter-current, via the inter-ference (the event): *the shortest distance between two waves is a sign.* This is what O'Sullivan has called "colliderings."

Compared to the magnificent hieratic credo of Bunting, "Take a chisel to write", O'Sullivan sounds our poetic a-anthem of the *Unofficial Word*:

> BEAT,
> **BELLOW**
> me Cloth /
> Shakings of chisel/
> Chounded all pitches

The shaking chisel (trembling, warbling, stuttering, faltering) marks a radical shift not just of aesthetic but ethic. The legitimate aspirations of pitch, not our tent, but our voicings. *Chounded*: a collidering of hounded, bounded, & founded with chow, with chew, what we eat in our mouths, the visceral words of the unofficial world we make by inhabiting.

O'Sullivan, in a 1997 interview, puts it this way: "… my work is driven by the spoken, sounded or breathing voice. Particularly I have always been haunted by issues of VOICELESSNESS—inarticulacy—silence—soundlessness—breathlessness—how are soundings or voices that are other-than or invisible or dimmed or marginalized or excluded or without privilege, or locked out, made Unofficial, reduced by ascendant systems of centrality and closure, configured or Sounded or given form & potency; how can I body forth or configure such sounds, such tongues, such languages, such muteness, such multivocality, such error—& this is perhaps why the non-vocal in mark & the non-word in sound or language—make up much of the fabrics & structures of my own compositions."

O'Sullivan's words lead by ear. Hers is a propulsively rhythmic verse that refuses regular beat; an always morphing (morphogenic) exemplum of Henri Meschonnic's distinction between the ahistoricity of meter and embodiment of rhythm. But O'Sullivan's is less an embodied poetics than a visceral gesture: not an idea of the body made concrete but a seismographic incarnation of language as organ-response to the minute, shifting interactive sum of place as tectonic, temporality as temperament, self is as self does.

So often O'Sullivan avers syntax for axial iteration, *word / ord / wo / rd / drow*, as if Adam grooved on applets and sugarcane, always on the eve of being able. Naming, here, is an avocation, kissing cousin of invocation and melody.

This is a poetry not of *me/me/me* but *it/it/it*.

Ecopoetics as echo-poetics.

"Knots, whorls, vortices" – O'Sullivan quotes this phrase from Tom Lowenstein's study of the Inuits in one of her poems; this trinity is emblematic, not of O'Sullivan's forms but of her *stamp*. Which, in turn, suggests the connection between her project and the intimations of the archaic that infuse her poems: a cross-sectional boring through time, whirling the sedimentary layers into knots. The archaic material pushes up to the surface. Collage and pulverization are at the service of a rhythmic vortex.

O'Sullivan's engagement with Joyce, especially the late work, is both intimate (in-the-sounding) and explicit (in-the-naming). If Joyce's words are like refracting, crystalline black holes, O'Sullivan's are trampolines.

There is no rhythm without song and yet song codes the acoustic surfeit that is O'Sullivan's ore.

O'Sullivan's visceral vernacular: autochthonous verse, tilling the inter-indigenous brainscape of the Celtic / Northumbrian / Welsh / Gaelic / Scots / Irish / Anglo / Saxon transloco-voco-titillated strabismus. It's not that O'Sullivan writes directly "in" any one of the languages "of these Isles," as she told once, but that they form a foundational "force field" out of which her own distinctive language emerges, as figure set against its grounding.

"At this point, *they* merge & ARE."
[*Un-Assuming Personas*]

Native to the soiled, aberrant, aboriginality.

Dialogic extravagance in the articulated, dithrombotic, honeycomb pluriperversity.

You say utterance, I say wigged-in, undulating, wanton specificity. Utter defiance as language-particle pattern recognition system. Defiance as deference to the utterly present, actual, indigestible, sputtering imagination of the real as punctuated rivulets of fragrant nothings in the dark dawn (stark spawn) of necessity's encroaching tears.

The medleyed consciousness of these sounds, these languages, is made palpable in O'Sullivan's poems, which lend themselves to recitation, while resisting thematization. Her words spend themselves in performance, turn to gesture, as sounds wound silhouettes and rhythms imbibe ("re-aspirate") incantation.

O'Sullivan cleaves to charm: striating song with the visceral magic of shorn insistence.

— Charles Bernstein
New York
(2004 / 2006)

tonetreks

tonetreks

by Maggie O'Sullivan

Edvard Munch	(1863-1944)
Kasimir Malevich	(1878-1935)
Vincent Van Gogh	(1853-1890)
Claude Monet	(1840-1926)
Alberto Giacometti	(1901-1966)
Arshile Gorky	(1905-1948)
Mark Rothko	(1903-1970)

MELANCHOLIA

Over the fjord
hemorrhage of carnival colour,
fever in the northern evening.

A laden sun has purpled
the sea's pounding;
sorrow leaks
through a fistful of rock.

(It is useless to look for horizons):
his heart does not squander its
raw splendour
on such credentials.

His knife-textured face
presses its gaunt stain
into the towel of yellow hands.

His tensioned eyelids avoid

the sea in every corner
the sea
twisting jagged lilac.

MALEVICH

white on white

white square on white ground
white ground on white square
groundlight on white
white on light

white nothing
nothing within nothing
within nothing nakedness
white nothing
naked

nothing revealing
nothing reveals nothing
yielding nothing
nothing yields nothing

white ground on white square
white square on white ground
groundlight on white
nothing holds nothing white
nothing inside nothing
beyond nothing
nothing more
nothing beyond nothing

white on light

VAN GOGH

Out of the vinegar smoke, their large
irregular boned heads and shoulders
knuckle to a roundness.
                                    In the lamp's
supperglow, faces mellow to pale amber.

                                        Potatoes
burst their boiled skins. Steam lengthens
the leaning faces.
                        Sounds crowd the table,
scraping forks, plates and coffee pouring.

Beneath the effortless
drip of a clock,
a cough or voice
stirs the deepening olive.

In through the window,
the locked out night
pulls the stray
whine of a dog.

A draught razors in.

The lamp is draining its full yellow
into the olivedark mouth
                            of the soon
                                        silent room.

MONET

(i)

AN ARC JAPANESE

moves into   patient

reflection

MONET

(ii)

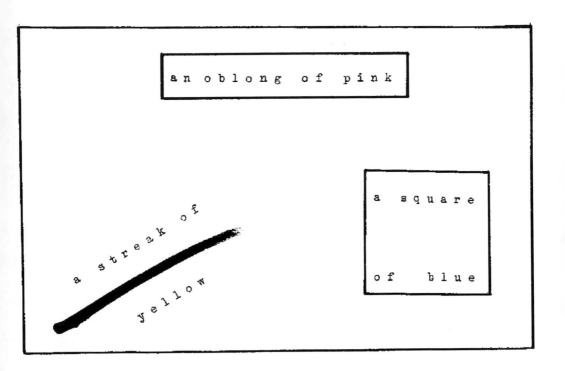

(iii)

PETALS PETALS PETALS PETALS
PETALS PETALS PETALS PETALS PETALS
PETALS PETALS PETALS PETALS
PETALS PETALS
PETALS PETALS PETALS PETALS PETALS
PETALS PETALS
PETALS PETALS
PETALS PETALS PETALS PETALS
PETALS PETALS PETALS
PETALS PETALS PETALS PETALS PETALS
PETALS PETALS PETALS
PETALS PETALS PETALS PETALS PETALS
PETALS

MASK   MASK

MONET

(iv)

your four

Paris

postcards

their lips

voracious

immediate

devouring cool water

GIACOMETTI

a
scribble
of
bronze
as
tall
as
we
see

he
strides
into
exis-
tence

his
bronze
flesh
spit-
twisted
to
a
sombre
dis-
tanced
skel-
eton

his
legs
thin
chiselled
and
arms

                his
            whittled
             almost
              no-
              thing
              face
          bayonets
              our
            glance
               as
               we
             walk
                  our
                  day
            into
                a
              crack

ELEGY

You measured things by weight.
You loved the feel & shape of apricots
the wave & sway of fields of grain
the strength & pressure of waterfalls
the flow & shimmer of rivers
the luxuriance of orange, amber & terracotta
on naked paper
the drift & wing, flutter & rustle
of birds & leaves.
You loved the surreal
the song
the edible
and, above all,
bread.

Your palette unfurls a flirtation
of glow & shadow,
a tenderness of breasts,
a poignant sweet incense of lemons
figs olives honey &
cherry trees in blossom.
The sanctuary holds all.
The bitter liver-red roses,
the scarlet-red crest of the cock,
the shivering silver sickness of poplar leaves
and the pallid hands, distorted, flat
as icons.

You said,
Permit me my making, there is no meaning here.
Meaning is the spectator's privilege.
The fetish
to invent a camouflage.

Surrounding the Connecticut farm,
the wave & sway of grain,
the summer twilight, tawny, violet-blue.
And you
dangling from a woodshed rafter.

ROTHKO

i

scent of
        stillness in the moon's greydrift

blurred rhetoric of distant thunder

slow approach of lit windows
quietness
tremulous black

the long walking   to the gate

        through the door
        corridors
        their plum complexities
                        lead
                to an immense room

grey tones call after me
                I hurry on
not wanting to get involved
in the drama of objects

                other rooms
                        full
of night bitten stillness
brooding   deepening
                to litanies of red vermilion

        wholeness of watching
    night's bouquet untighten

New York city climbs in through the pyramid of sky.
In the old carriage house
his bed table chairs and record-player.
Their gaunt tones echo
down passages
whose red complexities
rustle and deepen
to an orchard of plum.

Distance.

The first black
from the last black.

This. To discover as much
as the structure of a window
through which to feel the blurred rhetoric
of nearing thunder, the moon's greydrift.
To watch the night's bouquet untighten.
Annunciation of morning.

maggie osullivan

concerning spheres
maggie o'sullivan

To the Memory of my Mother

CONCERNING SPHERES

start, stop & build round its axis, a sphere
based on return.   by fracture or cleavage
of the melting point the fully liberated glance
is large enough to slip from side to side
of the sun.   when twinned & sinister,
this cobalt is widely efficient for use with
simple timings, i.e. measuring & extending
work still under the sea.

start, stop & restart by fracture or cleavage
of the sphere.   return to the axis its
curved form by liberating the lustre only
when the erosion is at rest.   bloom is
an important harness when the coating to be
measured is noxious & mispicked.   the timing
of such can be wedged to radiance without the
underground seams catching fire.   however,
due to the locked source of cockscomb reddle,
the tapering needles can be melted to measure
nickel streaks.   this operation so mingled
with impurities is timed to crater a star
whose metamorphic heat is never totally valved.

start, stop & build round its axis, a sphere
based on return.　　by erosion or rest of the
melting point the fully liberated lustre
is curved to ignite at a spark its own
gravitational zone.　　singly or in oblique
swarms, shafts are imported to envisage the
flast freed from air, to become amulets of
cosmic dust.　　in order to return to a credible
alloy, this operation must be measured & dripped
through fleece to yield a prismatic body
bounded by handling.

start, stop & restart by fracture or cleavage
of the sphere.　　de-fibre the crude, intractable
clusters from common orbit.　　the measurement
of powered cleavage is no solution, for the motion
of crystal & the capping of sulphur both return
hardily to the axis.　　for excavation purposes,
vertical matter is inadequate, for it hastens to fall,
while the pumping out of technique & symmetry
arouses to steam the bright bellowed gleam of
concealment so usually frozen.

start, stop & build round its axis, a sphere
based on return.   available either in rippled facets
or pyramids of carbon, the axis discharges enough
fire to depress some early beach.   its basic
refractions & reflections are brought down by the
action of its pinnacle at the last edge of colour.
without disturbing the overall timing of an absent
event, the sphere's need for air is loaded & raised to
surface in a weathering that cracks & terms its age.
thus diamonds of the first water are loosened from
such diagonal charges.

start, stop & restart by fracture or cleavage
of the sphere.   when the soft & hard alternations
of sphere are eroded to pebble, a spread brilliance
will return to the axis & the event will seem
to descend immediately.   release of this gain
at a smooth, partial speed will ensure its return to the
girdle of mythical use.   as the movement cannot be
stopped & will collide with its own curve, it is
particularly useful to lie in darkness since each
fleck of current gives timing a glint of diffidence.
while the measurement has immediately started, sandstone
& rose rock will have chipped & shelled the odd blemish
that swung out from their sequence & will have
rendered fertile the absence of the sphere.

NUMBERS IN WINTER

At once the fissured sea, sun bundled flush
of current. Gulled weight. Overhead, wax
confiscates motto, wing, beak, brow.

Aviation breaks & shines from these heaps
of perch & ear.

This not to be caged a memorable lilac banging
on the shallow shingle of winter.
Or a place hammered from another hollow nesting.
Billboards, or anenomes, the nightliest petalled,
slate. A taken kind of note.

And what of the eyes. Dave & his
heartache bring no harm to a walk like this,
here at the winding out of eeny meeny routes.

Aren't all steps joined by numbers to let in
the tumbled digits of wind & flood. Or a bowl
of yolks without a clasp to tremor from.

Now the hallmark fits. No squat history is
little.

What shelter overhead. And the Signora
connecting the most natural moments in granite.

Easy, the wisp of will between a decade.
From footage, finned marble delays morning.

Inherent in hands & other needs.
Accordingly, gladden abruptions, seal the
labyrinth, climb out.

JOINING THE COLOURS

g<u>ol</u>d

a feather, taken. though its brink of corn echo
survives, damned trick. well they paid for it.

careful where we step. heavy fun sets the wire
howling. a pelvic merry-go-round of tail,
fire. not pelt, yet aired with knife clean
heraldry.

stray stitches enter the lower key, divert this
pumpkin meat.

ah, the corner, indelicate angels. blown
muzzle, gartered footfalls, husks, mustard edge,
piss on sheets. not cuisine for those who
hold their stay against the light.

though at a pinch lemon-scented. lace stems
the underarm hair. a cloved dowry, its tarnished
weight reigns in the memory, a suburb of metered
city.

the champagne pageant dazzles still. a flex
of sun stretches from room to ruin. one false move
could plunge the lot in darkness.

amber

another condemnation. door chiselled pink from
fall. nothing to basket the change to cloth-pared
potions, a borrowed landing. shabby plumblines,
the sanded air making scale she says as she licks
the seasons out. a special trick for coining
hearts, the hurt bars of time in an itch of song.

a flight ascends, warm vermouth, this frizzle fibre
caught. young fox, running wood, flagged dead.
barleycup, a red so strung means yes, the mahogany
in mud, a gagged epilogue. a salient awe,
loomed to step in suede or grit.

evening acquires thickness, gestures assemble
in the dance. tendrils cut from each mistake.
she wipes back chrysanthemum canopies of must.

very bound from the dark, galaxies of moss &
stone folding intact.

emerald

perhaps matter of revenge. for the first time
direct access to the sea. a clear say found
in granite, a scoop of glaze or slate,
clippers inward. the birth of incorrect
equations, legacies pointed with care.

his need, iniative, a billiard room wanting a
shipwreck. a long tumbled touch of miniature
slipped in to change the pasture. the heavy
vapour of burning seaweed, cut from shallow ifs,
the tunics of prayer.

elevations & caesura. the process by which the
sea turns itself pungently away from event.

<u>cobalt</u>

again & again we touch the very held carriage
of nights.

a hail of recognition maps the route, chronicled,
chimneyed wax starting here to purple out the
stars. an anvil chiefly through seasons
of shore, shovelling the grey below the mesh
of sleep.

a new corrosion boards all miming.
any moment, had & then lost. any small
creature stalking the cracked dust of a room,
its armature brought down by a blast.
a telephone, longer than the blues.

a band staffed by sore Plush, their copious
pose formed from other species.
all enquiry has the configuration of a pea.
its fall to harm, offered not in this one
but in the one before.

conversely, we live in hope.

GROWTH

forehead. in the foreground. plot knuckling. out from the source.

    mouth. meshed timetables. ribs. emblems of place,
against the lungs. cheeks. eyes.   possible, but
easier on foot.

hour by hour. uncurl the body's gristle.

    search for hummings in the throat. borrow. recollect.
omit. etch a tang.

low & gradual. greyed irrigation.

    hair peeps through. a former place of siege.
root the thick brown differences. seed them.

dip to the clay's distance.

    unloosen the stones. layer. gain time. dub the sound.
hoop in an armful of little songs.

hint evenly. oddities repair the night.

    low-ringed. many small usages. the head a gravelly
burst. blob being pushed under. open to anyone.

lie open. prefer. tighten a brimful.

    flex the nerves. bare the retina. haul the shells.
    appease the grain. measure away the drizzle. learn
    to implicate the splendid jumble.

height and spiralled weight.

    a leash of tight yellows. smear the movement thickly.

a crinkled vein. a dark rosette or oval.

    threats neatened with turning. come. copious dice box.
    sometimes coloured. withdrawn to dry, cloistered
    remnants of winter.

down below the chewed skin.

    soft range. scent of clump. there, entry rustles the ear.
    speak from the firm side. the ability to rise is not
    needed. go. but don't annul the dancing.

the thought and surge of bud is real.

    trespass. deflect the tensile arches. stoop quickly.
    grasp, inhabit a story. spread the bouquet.

NOTES & OUTINGS

Listen.   Hear.

Exactly.   The exchange. This attempt to ask & say.
This talking from scratch, the rimmed indications of speech.

This talk will seem or not.   Long lined assumptions
crown out the fetching of words. Wounds image the
cellophane. Nothing to turn the chiselling.

Tearing can't wait.   Paper complexions, more green than
red.   Not bleak ornamental mouthing like agenda, statement &
report.   But imprecise, quizzical hazes like Drawing,
Passage and Poem.   Elements of a delicate, hooded tour.
Keying back to girlhood & beyond.   The rest too dry for
seed.   Surprise it.   Or let the diffidence in.

First then would be this.   It takes time.

The page split.   This the night we didn't talk.
Away from divisions & devices, there's a better need
to score the undertones, the something sometimes
heard.   Accidents invite a clarity that imbues the
fumbling with range and mood.

To restore the mass & stamina of early morning, it's
all down to the lowest point, the reign of change,
the wet and grey of chance.

Among other searchings, it's nearer still a trenching
of cold metal, an intake of holes.

Noon unminutes, day, a sequel to be watched, not
houred out.

It's me leaning from thrown windows to look at a rust
motor worn to bracken.   Or I can alter the programme,
turn off the light, pull off the pen, refuse to reveal
a position.

Relationships are possible, if boxed & emptied out
of drama. The neck, the chin, the eyes. Even
lashes do not answer unless they can lint in the
coming down on one hair.

To mix naturally, there must be no sluicing or
rimming the spillage.

They do not exist. Dropped edges. Except to garden
the tongue.

Glee & reach, the olives.
The white he's washing the stones with, or the sun,
brought back as a bonus. Or dogs who fight & bark &
fade to visitors who drop by to marvel & begin,
their badly worn details not always like this.

What you in your letter I'm starting. A matter of
going not of jumping. In this region it's possible
to push the lengths of braided cedar to my starting
point. The low used effects now chapped & remembered
all again.

The falling, not amongst other kids.   The walk home.
Breakage & coming together of cloud.   The concealment
of red-tumbled thigh.   I pick such givenaways & broken
things with a careful greed, taking one blade of each.
A regular flow can blur the search & run of pulling back
the pages.

I was one of the last. I staged the slim and large ones
in a language eared by the heart.   They slipped down
the narrow porcelain terms of the page.

A magnet unreliable.   For picking my way through
the slender voicings that settle obliquely at this
height.   Dawn, pollen tricked by wings.   Motivation,
a spiral newly built to bury nutrients not
understood.   Stone, pillar & path.   Below, the tipped
out cicadas, bay trees, old ones uprooting the yellow
stonecrop.

Lower, the sun leans & spreads and is the stealth
of heat & weed.   Preservation, a groove of grey pitted
steps.

Brakes engulf. Glaze of an alien alphabet.
Where are they taking what we fail to see. No food,
& yesterday's remnant, drizzles inflection
of rock on rock.
Wipers, cuckoos, our engine,
no a skeletal breath
high & cold on a cryptic
ridge of mist and road.

Betrayal, clues, echo. No directions
for this vertical
torque of drained deposits.
Procedure pierced by cloud, sleet,
we trying to catch
a carriage
of sheep & horses.
So near their gutted use,
they chain the route,
we fall away.

Elsewhere.
Remarks, accident, ascent from fog, a face however.
Retrieving, replacing (neither for nor against)
a vented dirt, the crossings. No sticky jargon now
to badge the snows.

Memory abates the gradual spring summit.
Still held, lights licking
the peaked head & spiral storm.

(May - Aug '80)

44

FOR MY MOTHER

slipsound papery
pake & her lash too
amidst rubbery beatn
      grey

        enemy thrift
             snowgood delicate
             ammonite keys
                   broken
            where clowned
                my head
             seeing

              one worth

a thousand
      hearings

     luminary
        womb drachm of gull
              crustacean

                  eyes want to mouth
           whatever chains
        detecting decking
         black dog
           deprived
       banished the blue
    i would impulsive
         power
           lip out my own

o yr light cut licences
take seat & last
all our puzzled ways

        itsnogood exiled angel
           dress
              divisible
        daubed brow borrowed grace

      & burned for me

now catch my thorns all night
my salt climbed currencies
      traced
        noughts of elder ground

   chuck out that orange

      get rid of the cats

    WOMAN
       we snatch passages
          of moth dribbled clay

if i your bones
         ALL
              so
briars kissed
      twice
half the dogrose
         ripened ones

                    whose very blood
              be cloth
                    came
                         in placings red

no falsity
      fits
           barking
    foliage fooled grey

                         nocturne coiled
                   the sun's notable gills
                              before noon
                         piebald squawking
                              bad
                         when they fly

         so sweet to lie
         among linen

REMEMBERING

flickering cucumber caught.
rose-red, how many gold hollow fire's breathing,
her stomach's crisscross winding light.

toes, feet, thighs, breasts.
radial the moment's wing to pass again through
change, the dark 24th hour, poised knife of a star.
plunged niche her breath feral, that laboured to touch
the skin's wrung fleece, pale sasparilla, dirt broken
heels, the soft fruit unthonged word. brevity veined
his/her step. the stone's fracture, facial iris
twined in flight.

cathedralled poverty, cleavage, the man, the blue &
loving tree. she waged correct, inert her wrapped
tongue a vase where peel of orchards hung, skin of
common toad. love bled packed wounds, buoyant the
bone usable minute & pillars imperative.

agape on the sill, eclipses of what ruggedness worn down,
reduced, akin to the linnet. combat mythical, the
main band black, abstinence, an estuary to become
extinct.

& what of

'the blackberries.   at the sight i

could cry.   not one blacked in,

amongst the whole bloody lot'

gorgeously she seared the house, locked small &
absolute rivers below the burrs & cadences of armoured
nerve.   she glassed out antics to talk of haunts,
& cursed him snow down broken tunnels of winter.
the lids held all & seemed to slip like sand or flow of
ice.   her just head bruising in the drawn clothes whenever
wet.   she snatched from the line, fields of some
knowledge brought with touch.   don't she said,
make fish of one and flesh the other.

mercurial her pulse in death cutting flight beneath
the head.   vigilant, a taste of angel real.
taloned oak, or moth, their number innocent as dusk,
their wings easing east a wind's balance to halt
magpies.   her comb's magnetic weight, illegible,
wilted fragrance, her curved intonation, the hand's
ragged paisley sprayed night & hem's locked wherever
touch paired with flint & frock ironed tendril.

waxed elm, red & brocade.   the bill said forever.
then in memory, the arteries blue dance, a state of
rain carrying principled flight.

'because of all the writing,

the same as a green field.

all the sods replaced.   keep going down

by the railings, until you find a man's

name.   this.'

TREE PIECES

<u>scots pine</u>

transgression

the cardinal shift from tongue to tongue

to calibrate the bough's legitimate favourite tree

total wood

white the neck's girth heart & lung the hourglass

coughing upward

spruce

nourishment

crustacean thickening the stain of dialect

skull & jaw

from chaos to damask

drudgery discloses the mouth's benevolence

rockface ribs impulse

rose fleece by starlight

<u>willow</u>

prevalent

caesura sheathed mornings upstream

each twig roomy stem commendable gliding thru air

ammonite or belemite

anterior

dilated mantle disturbance how cold the heart's

ablutions to music

UN-

ASSUMING

PERSONAS

MAGGIE

O'SULLIVAN

WRITERS

FORUM

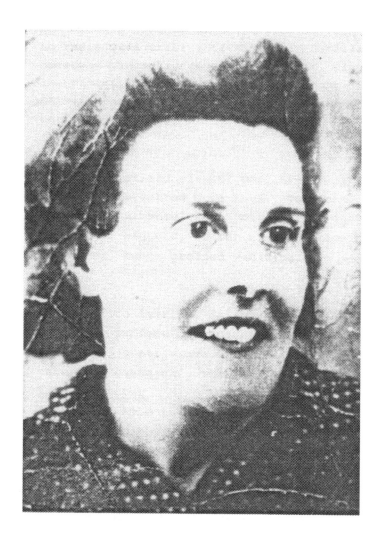

(dedicated to the memory of my mother)
(1912 - 1981)

HER cloth disTorted BROWsing FRAYing bark
to redisCOVER talk: intermission. Oscillations,
borrowed placenta, counting subjects, pinching
instrument, OVERthrown pedestal, tracks. Scanned
BEESwax, Bracken, Primitive Eye, Red of Rose
not in Rose itself.

HER mask: hollied plashof Oar. Grey capitals,
every fowl detected some nook. To Occupy
mutual disturbance, each celestial Weight of
gallantry: haggard, suddenLY clandestine A-
muse-ment, range groined vaulting.

HIS annulled latrine, daisy, focus, monogamy,
the rib's profane cryptograph, Orchid. NIGHT'S
fine edge, contrivance, accordant smallness,
results. Consequent, its Path Another.
Irregularities
introduced into that path, as reason sufficiently
dark. Hydrocarbon, concentric, the Breath
enigmatic, licked intrinsic, equinox & even
violet. The role of VIOLET, dim, compelled by
caprice, tracts of anomalous moment, Charged
Colour ReBUILt, Burst FOUNtain, ice, geography.

(2)

HER pace, melting mid-air chrysalis, spark &
wait recently as then. Thickets unLIT, stem,
inability, splintered furtherING, sleep.
Peripheral, spoonfuls of diction, alone the
hand reaching could bathe each twisted grey,
gill-slot, crown. Chromatic implements
pronounced 'bride' : pastime, pollen,
chlorophyll, dismembered terms, anagrams
among Teasel. Rash inference. Just to
kill rotational doubt, summons of earth's
hid, abyss amidst glutted slowness, BUT
not SLOWLY enough. The glow of snail, two-
together, linear methods paradoxical.
Acquaintance, Cowl from viewed silvery mist,
dimensions, to allude obvious measurements,
agitation in upper courts. To consider:
& the weakness be horizontal, romancing,
portcullis, habitations of Chases. First
dummy, proportion of retreat, Foliage,
Wound, Incised caption, LOSS.

HIS nearest limb, the act of transit.
Habiliments, almanac, circuit of surmise,
open, the body's brilliant Moons, GLUED
SUN.

(3)

Computations, Ncroachments, Mergence,
SNOW held converse, viaduct basIN, the drain
of cup, drop below square, swarmed rect-
ANGLES: hypothetical, devilled method, music
from little, nothing many pieces Broken.
Shallow hammer of source, touramaline, the
retina's myriad holdings. Obscuration,
velocity by fingers. To wear down & reduce
asperities. Tenanted. Words instead.

HER constant yellow messages. Reversal,
leopard, light & sweet skin, instancefuls of
threat. Causality lurking, yesterday dis-
SECTing nerve, removable, movably by screw,
the halves give image, complete object.
Curled resistance, the Tree-Black, half-
emptied tar & viral utterance. Excision &
infibulation. Hung in varnished blurs, place
indelibly another memory, blue soot, baled
prostrate.

HIS waves coddled ash. Decorum & sobriety
pitched by faction, brown gait, the backed
tongue. Cornices collar cleated brand never
more stuffed with scurrying, more decorative.

(4)

To travel the same principle as teeth that
pass double journeys of movement by window,
a day, a house in year. Aerials smoke,
collect conveyance, a single night drawn
black, the possibility of a few words
addled, pleasure, the surface refreshed.

Utility Opens shadow, Eyes rouge & else,
played for amazement, art.

Fomentation, powdered grievance, by need,
V-shaped poker filaments, marriage/versions
of marriage. Do limbs follow thought?
BigNESS? An even taste, orientation,
ridge of inexact, wilful logic. Adulated,
chewing tongue & cheek as if Lime slaking
there, slaking.

HER typographical strip, winter obligated,
so many nature's piled in ring & shackled
pose. The scale to which purpose is drawn.
Magnitude, pieced lead, a cushion, each hand
the same height, the most minute precautions.

Nail in wall, against clipped A large key:
thus locked, the door, by classic Am-
phibious effort, a modest LOW catastrophe.
Befitment, cells, a knot's tied plain pallor,

(5)
chimes of thunder. Behind gallop, what-
ever elevation came Seconds time.

<u>HER</u> adorable importance of naming/mis-
taking mauve press of months, remembering
at night, age, time of record, woman.

"<u>HE</u> shot & missed & called this act, <u>art</u>".

Awesome containment, the rotation of
music underneath her body. Leaning back,
terrible adjectives, nothing <u>out</u> of. In
each room: from One, deliberate passage
heard, from the other, a necessary Event.

<u>HER</u> registery, as is the ageing body disputant,
directly how related to this, fierce memorising
daily, even Hourly, beyond control, the canal
through centre.

At this point <u>they</u> merge & ARE.

Almost, erupting fullness, never wholly enclosed.
<u>HER</u> name retained with fern, rush, water. Plash,

(6)

concussion, vinegar nor Oil nor Critical
juncture, whose turnspits in concert,
careered regard. Asserted expenditure,
the Angle her impassable lily & devoted
lips, mentioned the point of termination.

Commodious HIS removal, whose charms
fortified the loophole. HER deep embrasures
& recesses, passed quickly as they came
convictions that her Eyes had not deceived
her: how discernible the mass of horn, its
election to tell of this.

Some weeks, magnitude applied accuracy,
firmament, in case what came the weariness,
which else, Ceres, Pallas, Juno, Vesta: the
gated Entrances where taken, the dew defeating
as it would, the still hidden flow.

Calamity, detection, detection, but never
fire setting the thin curtain of cloud.
HER column stains, carrying the sounded
abyss as guide. (Avert to inflict arrange-
ment away from BLOOD, smell of): she cared
not to comply.

(7)

HER face, water & food held out,
generously verging on who she was. That
manner. Rocking as though after madness,
her great arms rubbed windows, wrapped
arabesques in lard. A step downward,
heart repleted. Not to move leaf, nothing
more, her head fire walking, to globe the
world & know it as a province miles away.
She did LOCK things, her boneless good,
her drained selves: possessing no source
of illumination, is it lost for ever?
Predominances. Taken at interval, minutes
beneath a destitute boast: the scented
view, a different character. An aperture
enough to allow resplendent forenoon,
the loveliness of import, the clear
water dyed BLOOD. Tons, not pounds of
crust: the spot picked & fastened with
buffer of metal, degree of meridian,
superincumbent heat. But some heat.
Bricked virtue, velocity, to connect
this slowness between amusement.
Vibration again Arc of length, length,
ninefold so quickly the time of oscillation.

Elevation at midnight, veritably a wanderer
is.

(8)

The legate deaf to menace or promise.
"Vermeer's wife had eleven children".
The power of speech from shock dilates.
Sometimes she entered, partially, his
shadow. The moment first detected, to
watch its gradual encroachment. A scar
borne glare venting sleep: perfidious
insignia. Motto in RED, the central
gorged swan. Immolation from no climb,
tears leashing mouth, deviance not
locations of tepid move, cumulative,
away & chill constructed. Often HIS
noticing HER black drop, her hull, no
little delicacy, the gartered mantle,
surcoat & hood of interior continent.
To compute altitude to the end of shadow:
mere love engenders the fabric.

Late passages of torchlight, what name left
loose, dawdles initials, loops depth, water?
Epoch of object understood, the bulked
circuit of appearance to threaten or
destroy each of the dot's a Night's
observation. Foraged abruptions, birch &

(9)

plane equilibrium. Winter haemorrhage,
'coal-sack', dark lines of procession,
discrepancy an ordinary marble unique.

Musicality the sole method, capable of
manner, HER disturbance, attraction.
Fairblown, superstitions, licquorice &
algae & wild pansies, elongated, the two
cases edge muteness. Of intermediate
length, the lintel of door covering the
last few lines. Though not of whole sud,
ritual, wick, remission, crumpled abbatoirs,
a blue scum between hatred, the drainage
a trivial narration.

"She refused her eye, lest she should see
& be convinced".

HER stooped clover, sky blue or electric,
permissable secretions. Colonnation.
Occultation of star, iron-grey vertical
passages, night after night happiness
arrested. Running under the viaduct &
he outside of her. The door of recess open.

(10)

Neck. In last play of decay,
reconciliation, a gullible savaging.
The hen's claw, aperture, beak & ligament.
A row of corbels & parapet encountering
dragon, the condition of siege. Pliable,
flute cosseting paper: RED squawking kite.
Nearer & nearer bending towards the same
march of falconers, the rise & fall of
bird upon the fist.

These characters making possible.

HER motionless, big lettered lip an
upper gate open: its battlements &
towers, the excellence of lung in time,
the crescent again resumed preference for
place.

HER place, a juncture against his: mountain
mixed with matter numerically a comet. Sour
& damaged skill in any house, the listened-to
velocities of recollection, drawn from above
the knee, at rest mutual annihilation to
resist the guidance of attraction. He
strolled to her position. Elongation, foci.

{11}
What shape memorable?   The consequent,
elliptical path moved in curve.   A blue
hare, a fox creeping into the circle of glass:
then eagle entering both, presentiment,
reddish-brown misanthropy.   Love for
instance.   Thorax & flower, she lifting
up hands to it: afterwards, the BROW shards
to Zero.

A NATURAL HISTORY
IN 3 INCOMPLETE PARTS

MAGGIE O'SULLIVAN

CONTENTS

PART ONE INCOMPLETE

PART TWO MORE INCOMPLETE

PART THREE MOST INCOMPLETE

<u>INCOMPLETE</u>

<u>("Show me your face before you were born" - Zen Koan)</u>

The Moon's w/BLACK BLACK eye of wasp/BLACK black
Vanilla Scent. Skin of Open Fields, the. The Body
wringing odd skittish foreign public, fuschia lacewing:
Credentials Green, very floated lilac axle
pennyfans, filth-fold. addled quackery. lash capitals.
bonnets crinkle beat, lemon root shell bandeau
matched w/sand twinkle, seam: cheeky pulse & cheery
vertigo worn w/remix, Diffusion. Face prow. Bubbles.
Baffled Carne, cleeze w/fire echo. Vomica, primary
tea, see Skipping X. Flagjar, frecklebed, wintergreen
anyway, look...

Boulevard.

Fire, as in
the Sun.

promontory.
stroking.chaste.jade.stray.krakka.dash.chlorine.inflatable.turquoise.

Point.of.GARDENIA/steeped.MINT.Bedum.Lash.Mantle.
delphinium.Night.shot.
into.the.Skin.of.

shilling.tissue.diadem.moth.form.mimeo.courting.purple.blade.of.

Crockets.Angulate.An.

drizzled.voltage.trailing.arch.w/mesh.BLUE.fret.turning.butterfly.An.

Octave.fromz.peeled.or.lime.berry.blue.WATERING/Breast.SPACING.BLUE.BATHE.LANGUAGE.White
water.Go.Water.Go.drape.Bamboo.sidling.Button.Tincture.Addered.Thread.Sign.Blue.teem.
husky.Plunge.Go.Okra.PULSING.rind.pear.vein.&.Beat.Fuschia.Edge.tart.ice.&.BEAT.

milky.sulphide.cameo.
greenish.Aftermath.mallard.of.

Rain..Before.Dawn.

73

GOLD.intending.BLUE.in.

creamer.corrosive.zinc-weed.(cosm).stim.steep.maisy.BUT.BLUE-bluest.Daily.nightly.fetch.
anthem.device.fetch.mali.dip.dissolve.disarm.decoy.spatter.Blockade.shanty.shine-hush.
PROW.peddling.ash-dirt.sail-coal.COLD-pylons.mouth.formations.always.did.rock.phlegm.rock.
cherry.rock.crating.melt.rock.coltsfoot.arms.maizy.sank.Reverses.(GRAVER).oleander.O.gangs.
make.gigglish.kinter.make.fire.dins.make.lime.make.luta.lul.wash.make.wort.make.dins.make.
GRAPE.Diverses.Dye.Stomach.too.

. scold-struck.melt.incline.dip.gate.goes.fruit-scent:air.opal.desette.FLAUNT.each.blot.&.
. blur.torrential.almond.kiddler.night.MOSTLY.BLOOD.CRISP.mostly.veil.couch.wick.in.vert.&.
coil..b/ween.shudder.burst.several...

sour.then.dullens.DARE.powder.&.piece.&.jelly.&.puff.SAGE.pull.E.tin.blare.jarr.salt.
howlings.the.way.shoulders.FLUID.sill-viche.w/clotting.saw.hood.celanel.glox-lift.SKY.
&.go.down.jet.violet.underwater.signs.

LOOSH.MOONLIGHT.CRAB.

toe.folding.airs.
blood-burn.blood-burn.in.dirt.&.

firegig. screech vessel, far syllabub. at first,
gangrene cassava chewed green graft maroons pressing
filament, stroking.

stem.twisted.rare.beads.banner.&.jaw.how.blast.hit.
skin.burning.fire.like.necklace.tight-groundish.food.
hair.street-strumming.CALYPSO.blue.jolt.blackish-sage.
bibbed.morning.bled.PLEASE.even.stair.seams.artic.
thorn.ten-together.from.jangling.crib.&.ribs.damage.
gown.gone.jostled.doorswung.ochre.GONE.trinity.struck.
tin.rations.(LOVE).a.woodbine's.red.rare.fried.middling.
blood.cabbaged.cadence.shovelled.madrigal.kettle.song.

daytime.tema.looped.downwards.Blooded.Splash.with.
colonies.diamond.woodland.crinoline.Military.Rosette.
grazed.NOCTURNE.near.relative.the.name.rooms.cake.
the.care.w/which.pain.taking.the.turn.from.spelling.
SOLDIER.wearing.shadow.preserve..stone.the.night.
is.in.the.open.body.chalk.mostly.little.mostly.marginal.
mostly..............a.clock.spring.false.ion.ionist.
flower.step.by.step.carrying.brow.blue.or.blue-violet.
arch.to.sweeten.palate.arch.rye.carrying.the.

carnage, coin hemmed crucial peach, worse got willingness,
bless contorted font, cry strata, carpus the metacarpus:
lilacs injure incite rise
                    neck flare, mouth until

ever Hills, or mountains.
the

                    blood.that.morning.dipping.slits.
                    darned.poppy.orange.realistic.
                    Oranger.

                    ming curdled orchid:

vital.Orci.Orchid.wheels.gold.Bloodleather.Reels.White.Mountain.White.Frog.White.Ox.Hammered.White.Bridal.Spur.Wet.clove.teddy.screw.mustard.silk.milk.weeds.marsh.or.spot.pollinia.Watches.to.colour.brandy.green.of.open.fill-thin.Bog.FenHarvesters.Hard.Ha.ski.plumsbolt.swatch.salt.coral.sexual.syrup.Fur.polish.it.is.MICRO.fan.mangoes.vein(window)s...INTO.LIP.the.bee.fails.eye.eye.to.another.rotated.flag.dye.pulpish.sperm-spat.Lovesong.burnt.inside.Tresses.Twayblade.creeping.yoghurt.do.o.do.floppy.Lap.found.high.clutch.tribe.one.with.two.linings.scrubby.flowers.boat.RED.no.nectar.mix.allay.or.heal..NARROW.thought.be.rare.instead.the.white.heavy.shade.of.beach.by.means.of.dark.RED.sticky.mass.LUNACY..in.dune-slack.in.bud-glasses.in.bud-purple.coloured.alcohol..in.Earth-clips.inventing.magics..in.deep-lying.bloom.in.lollipops..part.of.theLip.tripping.Spurred.Coral.the.shoot.&.part..But.in.the.woods.the.brittle.spread.beneath.light.ketchup.notice.it.the.railway.verge.when.touched.JULY.the.lax.damp.creeping.of..BUT.it.shuns.more.heavily.TRESSES.the.crawling.forward.it.spikes.itself.in.vending.bronze.lower.down.it.once.grew.it.once.grew.BELONGING.figity.grounded.brittle.plume.caramel.to.

Crudely reddish red yellow
sedge under bridge, gold in
river, cut w/crushed vein,
stabbed running reeling
usages, notably.

in happy Yellow lies light
not so much
        leaves, it is & strapped,
volume, this (towards the)
saying of, pushing soil,
(towards the) saying of,

                (towards the)

Vassal. madrigal. django reign blistering navybricolage.
Decayed Beam, ski tar pulls thigh, runs thick lesion:
scratching, dancing, mixing, aX another

when suddenly

codices & flay lavish cinder brooches mark brow of black's
dominant prone total cloud, cast quick FLAKE hemming
curr: render batter sea his fatally pierce, cut raspy
churl. Choice open globe, (su-burb. prowl. some size.
prowl-mitt. be.nuss. kid.ease).

MirrorBall.
BEING LAID.
Sans Soleil swan simplest whispering sumach, arm's cold
lustre swole Tango Pulsing. drill grill. Boogie glacis
fooled finial saliva, reflex of immediate immense cry.

describe.
Thunder. Bleeding. The Sky Confessing It.
& being
jobless.

Billow churn, jazzy curve. Bee zen. of Glovewort.
Utter Glaze. fridge roseflocking mutagenic. fridge Acanthus,
lash prim thistle twist of pure nutmace, low flambé lead
split: erosion. But child, Bead & reel, yellowed air soft
mightily, i bleed & soak & pool olive, prolonging
sund sund sundering

real rain.

Pollen.Primitive.Sting.Hatch.Firebrat.Tubular.Realm.Phose.Pest.
Ant.Anatomically.Furnace.Infernal.Warm.pigs.Pipes."Know.Feelers.
Noise.Green.Glanding.silk.or.Venom.Wasp.Antennae.Lock.Button.
Earth.The.Next.Step.&.Seal.INSECT.INSECT.INSECT.INSECTS.Bumble.
Bees.Butterfly.Moths.Brine-fly.Wellheads.Weevil.Water.else.
Spring.Field.GrassHopper.Distant.they.as.Great.Air.to.find.Lo.
Locust.would.be.longer.Longer.Fly.Beetle.Mosquito.Suck.third.
Cylinder.Mine.zone.Certain.seeps.Air.peed.Pale.Green.Butter.
House.Wasp.Hornet.Honey.Horse.Pupate.Longhorn.Winged.poor.
starch."joined.feet".Anthro.Arise.Appendages.Bristletail.Or.
Organs.of.touch.proper.legs.BODY.SECTIONS.stride.bearing.
wingless.thorn.Nectar.wing.cannot.fold.wing.their.wings.walk.
&.thorn.&.climb.Grasscry.Mayflies.Dragon.Cock.Cicada.Beetle.
others.Fossilfly.Earwig.Seeping.White.pine.bit.of.tiny.tan.
mite.Sarcophagi.Banded.Fire.Stag.Horned.She.Twig-flight.Grub.
to.wing.form.Pale.&.ate.&.sea.Solid.sap.Tasting.a.Daisy.Dusted.
Green.Lines.loom.ordinary.honey.burrow.Goldenrod.Nips.its.prey.
Bits.Insidious.Prime-gut.Those.does.Diptera.Speck-suck.Arachnida.
tick.spy.spy.my.my.speck.legs.Daddy.Thousands.of.small.complete.
EYES.Steer.sun.Strike.eye.to.Doom.Mouth.pats.abundant.hair.to.
parts.bend.appendages.Fuse.ganglia.Nerve.calls.Mound.acuity.
Corneal.Red.looks.that.glow.Whip.tympanic.Stridulate.Sand.chirp.
Snare-drum.No.true.voice.Creak.Creak.Moon.lights.wing.rasp.
filly.vein.spur.Honeydew.drip.crop.clean.combs.Visited.oil.fun.
finicky.link.to.cab.nasturtium.bedings.of.the.hair.lift.ball.
fuzz.Oriental.the.white.those.in.air.praying.Mantis.maxillae.
coil.blood.mandibles.bite.sight.stylet.Heart.&.Poison.tubel.
Pyloric.fly.ord.(A).crop.complicated.mouth.houses.prismatic.
feathery.feelers.Sole.sole.on.wing.tiger-beetle.snout-meat.
Syphon-scent.half-zipper.does.the.work.cuticle.hook.&.eye.
halterers.More.flap.An.aphid's.birth.decade.painted.lately.
coming.habit.nymphal.moult.g.g.finally.wing.such.queen.quick.
blade.stem.cracks.ASSIGN.all.the.time.Spotted.Swarming.Faster.
gregarious.Winged.Monarch.into.four.fur.thin.velvety.tightly.
to.two.did.not.raw.could.Flow.Canker.Handmaid.Harlequin.Place.
to.hid.to.hide.Junkyard.of.A.slit.comb.unit.of.beebread.even.
pebble.porch.ovals.of.Thousand.Ovals.Leaf.Be.B.Begins.Build.
Another.Mix.Begin.a.new.Dauber.Vaselike.Wasp.Each.ineach.See.
Sealing.Pebbles.in.the.first.fist.Caterpillar.an.eggg.it.Thin.
cuticle.as.temporary.mate.Queen.Soldiers.Qoe.Worker.Primary.
Hind-Gut.Valve.valve.VALVE.Hatchet.into.heat.nest-fret.Gain.of.
carbon.White.ant.Hexagon.Saliva.Tool-using.WASP.Leaf-Roller.
Caddisfly.Cylindrical.Inch-brick.Ambrosia.Tap.excrement.Soft-
wood.bark.insects.into.jaw.into.Snap.dune.Many.times.Moth.larva.
teeming.deadly.partial.back.teeming.predaceous.Game.of.catch.
bee.flies.rob.flies.robby.Ladybird.Cliff.edge.abdomen.periodic.
sting.Black.&.yellow.unpalatable.caterpillars.Pillars.Exquisite.
cerise.perfect.sum.Resemblance.to.gaudily.birch.decor.as.Puss.
Moth.Milkweed.Four-Eyed.Bug.Shade.to.Discourage.ENEMIES.Spined.
Poisonous.Honey.Sparks.inDark.Four-Pointed.Shot.Pattern.Hurry-
ing.Only.Eye.Comb.Propolis.Stung.load.their.tongues.bee.wags.
Waxen.See.Sell.Clinging.to.Wing.Condition.Root-laced.mud.Dragon.
Damsel.Caddis.Nay.May.Mosquioto.sub.soaring.wrigglers.Skating.
whirligig.Backswimming.Waterboat.to.take.Silver.like.Breath.It.
has.to.Stray.line.tool.too.a.clutch.keep.duped.culex.wings.awhir.
awhile.Instinct.In.lay.for.it.Nest.Roof.Honey-Carnage.rend.a.

brickettes iron & stand river rioting ledge looking.
Eye caught face lay neck & wrist, lay flank & paddle
bloody veering eye matching internal gash mix, hell met
below the tongue, pulling down (i shadow) glan break
ginger jarring Black talk blood come tallow naming bleed
w/finger be shudder burst be Furnace Rap nil nil rip
ease, Mix. grassa promptly. Else gloo buff, Else. Straw.
some slant coking gladi chronic yellow. Loosey dug
tendering. Slay labour crunch Drumming howl w/bite &
string Blood
varnish,
torrential plume

RED
RED
winged
RED
RED
Recurring
Corney
Beat:
Denier
vexing
Denier
vexing

clove tone, warpage, trampling joy guard. trigger
elbow

armouring

curve, get rag/

      time

        no ordinary

     meaning RED

     the basic daily requirement:

              GROUND RUCHE lung/knit w/KNIFE
                  Weep Crockery & bind.
                       BLEED.

                         (from which no

single cut

snow division
blade hover many blade

w/foot ringing light & burn banded wing bird mix over
speed of wood w/flock distant land tumbling yellow circles
frightened mound over head mouth to mouth into sea.

slippage, mirror.
flecked scalping (flame hue) inflict
lemon. trace, trace bespattered clashing rib, RED Lock
Multitude. Locks Black Bluish Black. Locks curl razor
down womb shooting taupe rotted solvent/Tongue posse
done w/NOW. done w/.
done w/claw loaden keel,
done w/FIRE down the spine,
done w/GUT blooding down ashes.
Ashes.
done w/larken shot.

done w/this my BODY,
done w/this my BLOOD,

done w/this my

how birds flock to
the primate world, how

livers PELT mocca gut & MARK pearl sauce,
attach PAIN'S GREY PERMANENT WHITE READILY

1. accustomed as.
2. DID.
3. rooms double use.

                    lastly,
          delineate invisible trains & Broken sign
   flaps
     in breeze
         hanging line
     crippled rope of stumbling

            the head,

            how to.

            _____

MORE INCOMPLETE

("If love Be not in the house there is nothing")-

Canto CXVI

- Ezra Pound

Magenta powering carbon finch: hawk's veil.
Kale crimson star felled linen. crag mumbling
claw. Lily. Twisting pebble & SILENT
Red becoulding curtsy.
Carrier.
Blood Ivy.
Julep.
BLOOD/smudging palm & tallow drown
mussel BOATS carry. And ABJURE.
And Pain.

---

sigil.
porch.apostrophe.
INCISION'S

    Bred Blue EARTH-LINT, lick
 an curr an root an drum an string an knife an hum an
haunt an womb an TELL sick sickle asterisk.

Saffron cloy, grapey clow/Reddish MONDAY.
Gram straw, bed pebble, plantlet runway rooting
tassel juice, Doom choc, Impulses.
Let/White laugh. Love. Love lantern. Dance touch,
Grave Appraiser

streaming bloody pungent/thru dark purple holly blue
underwing/HOWL high thigh treadle snout, wornly, having
stoop. Having stoop as that of hare, as that of lion,
as that of canticle, cordico, Slate.

---

skips & scrim. chickling HEART littering teal
eye Black lid willow ran BLACK/BLACK

Breathful
,breath .

rim belly BLUE/BLACK w/skin gone barley root so red so
flickering BLAY BLADE ASCENDING BLADE helming vertigo:
garm baggage, date can, lodge cream rib-leaved cake
flimmering clatter:
CALM grease
gutting poise
kohl sunken

wire

cadmium bend & shut scatter base berry nickel
Rose open skin
kindling

SASH CARNAGE

carob kerbed silk pulsing scald hung in cloak,
own cloak heather lurk w/quilt broth, w/Crab Veil
wristing raw, w/lace bound Eye-rift, w/Emerald city,
that. That Brine.
        ribbons/lacerate,
            thread

    such

    lamentation

such (WILL RESUME)
such glide, Inductance.

such green simples.
such

& meadows any.

Eareye. Eareye line glue & hum along Blue marm/bee
sheety zag

   BLAY/

   BLAY BLADE ASCENDING
   BLAY slash & ribbon, snare lish bloom
lee littoral slow frame iris to Ocean Posy wilding on/bingle
breaking vinegreen:

radial.arm.saw.shellac.Hazel//saw.decoy.(knot.&.glove).
doughty.hume//saw.clerken.whirl.terra.visca.CLAW-YARD.
claw.bouncing.heel.Ovette.anvil.skit.painted.Blax. X/
PLODE

    (instructions for Breed)
   & sit by me & sit by me clutching
        REPEATED)

Glamour Still. Count S. pain. Black tie tender dumbling
scar-curdBLACK show go pink/KNIFE is BEING & BLOOD is.

is BLACK

     truest
     ASH
     hung
     MoonFOOTAGE,
verti pillow slid rocks lace blue Leapt haw ruched
throat neon, ruched root cleave on skin's garbling
hearse. Mud lattice. Moor Pitch. Black-a-Purple.
Sombre savage tangles tilling

PURE BRIDGE

Utter Gravel.
Gravel utter slow ska tanta blouse brindle stemming
core: saffron tarmacs rip sheet whites, go stem
rudge cardoman from bare knee kneeling bare swarms
red wild dippled heat & vertigo, Peep Robes &
Cot Common Peel. Poppy Bone.
Pen Herds
prowl curve w/wrist gown
        w/tin alight
        w/graphing forrest
        w/weeding shove

grave (noisette) across marble
(or choking)
dead slow
(jangle) from
broken Fields broken,
prong w/icy lamming bone, Daisy.

Snarl carvels loom calico & go Sapphire swift on
frown pitch, on lamé orchids, cotton, skin. One.
Unspeakably.

Water.collected
as in marsh. or lake.
the hills lead to

(for my mother)

Inland Further. limpet. mandible. lapping Lovely:
Partial rue gem, para-gauntlet. Sizzle mezzlar,
w/hand drawn Jam Air ascensions. Spinal Rose/
Mullein Absolute, blush bleeding loom her Copper
blind/my Black ripple, sedgey spring, snow Tattoist
w/grieving edge,
w/SHARROW.

Real Rain. Whole veil of
Sky.

flare
black
into

whale-thing, hawthorn herbed shawl, Recurring kiss,
Redempting metal

                    name enja/

Arrow match leadley bannister, rinding visage, red ludge,
Brackeen: Drop grinding buckle nib, strawberry w/out brake,
scribland WOBBLING croon rouge, twine ragging lamp:
Poppy patter, torn creosote, meaning NET/NO DRUGGIST.
Peel tender Mother
Delving

            (like noBODY at all)

                    (like noBODY at all)

wish WE.

(could WE not)

WE
AFTER DARK
floor sag Day/Bet Rose can tenderness, can turn, can.

/UTMOST SONG/
/SCATTERING FLUGEL/

        Raise Fire Forrest as Wood as Molecules of
        the AIR itself.

Mammal without end.

dereliction.

              The Art of Silence.
              _____

(for my dad)

collarless.kith.have.crept.&.humped.the.Madder.in/Buttercup.Field/gartered.sugar/temper/Cutch.
a.stubbled.figurine/Fractured.lard/Fractured.leg/Stuff.soil/Gruff.ecumenical.stirring/Postillion/
mackerel/tri-colour.Bard.gathering.threepenny-three-no-more/threepenny.Irish.elder.flitting.

STUB.SKITE.&.CATCH.THEM.CAUSAL/John.L/caraway.Cork/LOUD.F's.&.BLINDING/boot-nail/mutton-vestment/
WILD/gentle/WILD/meridian.January.slunk.slung.elliptical.daddle.

JAR/Dogrose.ifs/poplin.clog/poplin.crow/jowl/crow.the.spirit.in.OR.out

nay.NO.dribble.daubed.motley.host/
BUT.inlaid.stouted.sharp.HEIL.or.swung.plum/he.spittle.gentle/CROW/
jowl.&.Crow.&.wild.gallons.

he.BLACK.BLACK.Rebel.he.

```
THIS.IS.RED.&.THIS.IS.PINK.THIS.IS.RED.&.THIS.IS.PINK.
THIS.IS.RED.&.THIS.IS.PINK.THIS.IS.RED.&.THIS.IS.PINK.
THIS.IS.RED.&.THIS.IS.PINK.THIS.IS.RED.&.THIS.IS.PINK.
THIS.IS.RED.&.THIS.IS.PINK.THIS.IS.RED.&.THIS.IS.PINK.
THIS.IS.RED.&.THIS.IS.PINK.THIS.IS.RED.&.THIS.IS.PINK.
THIS.IS.RED.&.THIS.IS.PINK.THIS.IS.RED.&.THIS.IS.PINK.
THIS.IS.RED.&.THIS.IS.PINK.THIS.IS.RED.&.THIS.IS.PINK.
THIS.IS.RED.&.THIS.IS.PINK.THIS.IS.RED.&.THIS.IS.PINK.


THIS.IS.RED.&.THIS.IS.PINK.THIS.IS.RED.&.THIS.IS.PINK.


THIS.IS.RED.&.THIS.IS.PINK.THIS.IS.RED.&.THIS.IS.PINK.



THIS.IS.RED.&.THIS.IS.PINK.THIS.IS.RED.&.THIS.IS.PINK.


THIS.IS.RED.&.THIS.IS.PINK.THIS.IS.RED.&.THIS.IS.PINK.


THIS.IS.RED.&.THIS.IS.PINK.THIS.IS.RED.&.THIS.IS.PINK.



THIS.IS.RED.&.THIS.IS.PINK.THIS.IS.RED.&.THIS.IS.PINK.
THIS.IS.RED.&.THIS.IS.PINK.THIS.IS.RED.&.THIS.IS.PINK.
THIS.IS.RED.&.THIS.IS.PINK.THIS.IS.RED.&.THIS.IS.PINK.
THIS.IS.RED.&.THIS.IS.PINK.THIS.IS.RED.&.THIS.IS.PINK.
THIS.IS.RED.&.THIS.IS.PINK.THIS.IS.RED.&.THIS.IS.PINK.
THIS.IS.RED.&.THIS.IS.PINK.THIS.IS.RED.&.THIS.IS.PINK.
THIS.IS.RED.&.THIS.IS.PINK.THIS.IS.RED.&.THIS.IS.PINK.
THIS.IS.RED.&.THIS.IS.PINK.THIS.IS.RED.&.THIS.IS.PINK.
THIS.IS.RED.&.THIS.IS.PINK.THIS.IS.RED.&.THIS.IS.PINK.
THIS.IS.RED.&.THIS.IS.PINK.THIS.IS.RED.&.THIS.IS.PINK.
THIS.IS.RED.&.THIS.IS.PINK.THIS.IS.RED.&.THIS.IS.PINK.
                                              THIS.
```

same venue

Sun longing daze wove. mauve on twine lar. BLUEdiveable
wood wag shuffering kic. clothspull paining skin sharpening
Rose pitchy plum. alienist. whisht. whisht. plumey hoke,
brine-buckle of sweet huffy rim. Locks conflate. fugue
drool dyed heavy. Dangling period petrols chyle & brood.
Sky rasping runs nettle/EDGE of bramble/REAL jewel inversions
lid night, line artillery
w/CRY
w/CRY
w/CRY
w/CRY Darkish Jamson, monkish astor/Broken lid
meshing switchblade, meshing leaf's puckered oat: meshing
pewter brew, live round.
Lie Reverse.

CROW lenders indigo. Crow glag driven artery.
driven rope spinning varna, lone moth, drove Cranberry.
Torn centuary, femme peddlar sweatbloody crepe. Souffle:
animal tumbling thistle thru Tamarind. Plumjoy claw
amok til stain, amok til salt, amok till ribby lead,
til orange pits tear vinegar folds open, open:
kinda felt bap blood:
kinda fence-barb.
ISLAND searching touch, touch, touching,
each word word word wording
for weeks
PUMA-pepperpot.
glue-crane, SPY & sense
digi Blind & cloth abound. deportation

dishpan glass & bomb & gun & knife & fisty
brush of timber
DOUBLE strawbent, bowed
Body Oak/Egg Down, clad magnolia pansy froze/hinding
RED: grieve dress, chrysanthemum
shunt, fuse rune, SILVER
RED, snarling alphabet, enamelled Larkspur, hinge-
medicine: wail vestage
sill weed, chrome bone celandine, munch
ice pelled by bark, doom cusp lit by salt, by trudgey
moth, by laurel nurdling, how
to punch, how to voice, how to punch, how to voice for
FIELDS.

Forrest. Water. as in rain.
clouds. springs. streams.
and defiles.

till dawn. this morning.

ANGLE
OF BLOOD:

WARNING
SEA-PASSAGES:

PICTURES:

Orange.tip.step.&.looking.those.who.THOSE.WHO.under.gang.Under.
Ear.UNDER.cherry.stanza.dress.for.shooting.dialgo.voice.Muslin.
Leaf.Fork.thru.LIGHT.ARRANGEMENT.thru.children.thru.loss.thru.
damage.thru.theft.thru.the.nettle.afterwards

/the question of origin/

doom.flutter.(and.cheap).as.illustration.as.fetish.as.thing.to.
learn.tar-torn.abberations.Ailanthus.Wood.given.the.speed.with.
which.crawl.from.frass.Absorbent.tepid.'A'.Pine.sleeve.daily.
WHITE.LETTER.HAIRSTREAKS.white.folding.continuously.brooded.
White.flight.stinging.sleep.in.caves.(or.claspers).with.silk.
then.SEA.on.a.Cane.SEA.

/echoes/

Red.Ridge.Running.Random.Cage.Running.Cage.Running.Care.
single.stow/cudgel.straw.slouched.facing.straw.nasturtium.
Markings.of.comma/Markings.of.reach.Wych.Harrow.Common.Elm.
instar.or.even.solitary.metallic.(Doris.Red.Doris.Phyllis,
among.others).settles.will.feed.bright.yellow.taking.green.
in.song.taking.pain.in.mating.taking.TIGER.LIME.&.small.
copper.common.sorrel.SKY.COVERAGE.

/concern for repetition/

Docks.ringlet.leaving.ARROWS.IN.THE.BACK.honey-love.leaving.
sunny.mesh.LEAVING.Dog.Violet.&.OTHER.twig-low.honesties.
HONESTIES.haunt.&.heart.&.china.spots.on.the.tide.VERTICALLY.
a.rash.come.to.thorn/come.to.lay.in.chain/come.to.red/come.to.
mass.roll.laminate/come.to.scud.penitent.pile.of.rush/come.to.
halted.ice/come.to.dull.cherry.rime.jacket.on.red.backing.rime.
worn.to.front.rime.worn.to.red.

Twice.wavy.Helps.Buff.Straw.willow.to.outer.margins.(against.
which.the.wind).White.paper.oven.at.night.

Deports

WHITE.flake.WHITE.ivy.WHITE.

93

ElmZbank. LmZ. fraze.
doughty Laughing Puckered Choinage, Bossa. ta.
ble. Totem thorning breath Peacock, Prism Tango,
cavalcade. Juggling lakme, juggling
bip Blue Happen w/emerald
tacking deal, claw, tacking deal. tacking throng.
tacking.
lachrymal.

Jongleur,
fastening LAND Black/codling pull of skin/star thread:
setch raking shoreline, raking eye's violet
skew Black shift. Carve stem, Chess Wing, Sling trove.
jute hawking pelt. Keel beet in shellBLUE
frost. Keel blue
disorderly

drawn in by scar, waves
tap on the eye/moonlight
is
the pace.

is the pace ebonese.

Throat cruisa, carrier, stone
tracing spey sour mash/salt tracing Laburnum Reel Jar.
tracing Pan Jalta. tracing Movement. Pertillance.
BLACK

paysage/BLUE
readiness of it all.

Kyrie. Cara. Cushla.
cuvil, claw glossop, skeletal sacos, vaso, sharpish.
DONE drinking silk sequin burr, done eating oat,
DONE honey-tongue,
DONE vanish.
DONE.

SING in Scorpion/Tin Bramble Rocking/CRY
Spurge under Wing, cliff common Blue where wild thorny
Violet love had been White eye of Skullmilk, the.
The Skull,
embroidered Sheer BLACK/embroidered Purple strip
sting w/silver SKULL.
w/FLEET

Eye green roofing sickle arch, roofing weed,
wrung rag & string saffron lime subtifuge.
Whistles tauter, check whistles for
seditious
thistle/magenta nomad wrecked in
oil arresting: Aloe. Bold drome rind, harsh cordite,
GRIEF/stun substance. Ash weed dripping vein, gone
GRIEF, the Moon gone Grieve Eye
ROUSE Corpus. Basal acres Builded
Verde. Vern-
Ocular, O violet such, such open feather (curdling)
coral cocoa reaching

Constant smokey Fro Folz. O Red Mull. O netta stud,
astounding gel. Zanth guard, building seshting:
Brokey shoal dare, Crackled Sung, Damning Whirl/Building
flam lunge, skin hurt, hoop, hydra-garment, sacro-
tenses. O
Building.
building.
Say Machette, glay tinge, FLAW punctive, Red
Real
Wire cutting nettle swallow, knot scavenge, RAIN.
RAIN.

Slam in the seam/SINGE Cobra. Burr Flutt woollen,
hacked mauve/Blue & figure cry stood among reed/
(HOW STOOD)
How Heavy Hook Troop/pelt in cedar is, is Long is/
is DREW IN.
is.

Rag heel, common place of tidal pitch, GLASS
behind bars

                ,gree,
                jace,
                gun-wharf (the sequence that we learn
starts with)

                /could've...

        (lifting the ears away from

pitched phurnacite. Alger tilting Ragwort. Twin BLACK
& Moon rowting deal hung cane marionette. Knotting Sky
Thru yard/ thru glass / thru tongue / thru wing /
thru crop & crush / crop & crush / crop & crush/AGAINST

Disruptive patternBANNER material.

splinter downwards pullover blouse of a

FLAME. Flame sash over green Large lanyard blashly aspen
Red local rate of fire goblet. Hackle (& silver
(& silver (& silver (& silver
grip w/Eye
crimson cuff dripping round, close range, close range,
rick dirty tottering death to bad

RAIN RED light.

Blue combing yellow dominate. Dicebearing.
Barrel-tunic. Chest-button. Brace-powder. BLOWback.
bourbon dig ribbon. axe & shove. Chy pick w/no stars.
cake form, frog fix, pitch ankle sheer strum. sheer
bangle of low voice lying there, bent olive, underbricklet
of sheet, w/nil ground, w/nil ground,
w/nil
underneath.

97

Moral Conditions.

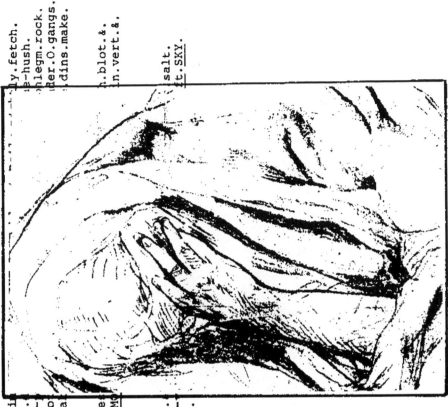

ly.fetch.
-hush.
phlegm.rock.
der.O.gangs.
dins.make.

h.blot.&.
n.vert.&.

salt.
t.SKY.

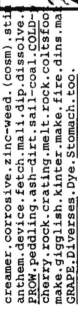

GOLD.intending.BLUE.in.

creamer.corrosive.zinc-weed.(cosm).sti
anthem.device.fetch.mali.dip.dissolve.
PROW.peddling.ash-dirt.sail-coal.COLD-
cherry.rock.crating.melt.rock.coltsfoo
make.gigglish.kinter.make.fire.dins.ma
GRAPE.Diverses.Dye.Stomach.too.

scold-struck.melt.incline.dip.gate.goe
blur.torrential.almond.kiddler.night.Mo
coil..b/ween.shudder.burst.several...

sour.then.dullens.DARE.powder.&.piece.
howlings.the.way.shoulders.FLUID.sill-
&.go.down.jet.violet.underwater.signs.

LOOSH.MOONLIGHT.CRAB.

toe.folding.airs.
blood-burn.blood-burn.in.dirt.&.

99

The Moon's w/ 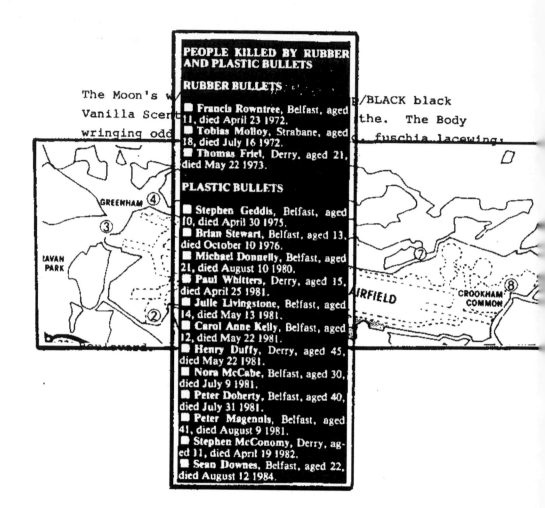 /BLACK black
Vanilla Scent the. The Body
wringing odd fuschia lacewing:

PEOPLE KILLED BY RUBBER AND PLASTIC BULLETS

RUBBER BULLETS

■ Francis Rowntree, Belfast, aged 11, died April 23 1972.
■ Tobias Molloy, Strabane, aged 18, died July 16 1972.
■ Thomas Friel, Derry, aged 21, died May 22 1973.

PLASTIC BULLETS

■ Stephen Geddis, Belfast, aged 10, died April 30 1975.
■ Brian Stewart, Belfast, aged 13, died October 10 1976.
■ Michael Donnelly, Belfast, aged 21, died August 10 1980.
■ Paul Whitters, Derry, aged 15, died April 25 1981.
■ Julie Livingstone, Belfast, aged 14, died May 13 1981.
■ Carol Anne Kelly, Belfast, aged 12, died May 22 1981.
■ Henry Duffy, Derry, aged 45, died May 22 1981.
■ Nora McCabe, Belfast, aged 30, died July 9 1981.
■ Peter Doherty, Belfast, aged 40, died July 31 1981.
■ Peter Magennis, Belfast, aged 41, died August 9 1981.
■ Stephen McConomy, Derry, aged 11, died April 19 1982.
■ Sean Downes, Belfast, aged 22, died August 12 1984.

GREENHAM
LAVAN PARK
Boulevard
AIRFIELD
CROOKHAM COMMON

Fire, as in
the Sun.

Vassal. madrigal. django reign blistering navybricolage.
Decayed Beam, ski tar pulls thigh, runs thick lesion:
scratching, dancing, mixing, aX another

of black's
hemming
raspy
size.

arm's cold
glacis
nse cry.

describe.
Thunder. Bleeding. The Sky Confessing It.
& being
jobless.

Billow churn, jazzy curve. Bee zen. of Glovewort.
Utter Glaze. fridge roseflocking mutagenic. fridge Acanthus,
lash prim thistle twist of pure nutmace, low flambé lead
split erosion. But child, Bead & reel, yellowed air soft
mightily, i bleed & soak & pool olive, prolonging
sund sund sundering

real rain.

Pollen.Primitive.Sting.Hatch.Firebrat.Tubular.Realm.Phose.Pest.
Ant.Anatomically.Furnace.Infernal.Warm.pigs.Pipes."Know.Feelers.
Noise.Green.Glanding.silk.or.Venom.Wasp.Antennae.Lock.Button.
Earth.The Next.Step.&.Seal.INSECT.INSECT.INSECT.INSECTS.Bumble.
Bees.Butterfly.Moths.Brine-fly.Wellheads.Weevil.Water.else.
Spring.Fie⋯⋯⋯.to.find.Lo.
Locust.wou⋯⋯Suck.third.
Cylinder.M⋯⋯en.Butter.
House.Wasp⋯⋯ed.poor.
starch."jo⋯⋯etail.Or.
Organs.of.⋯⋯earing.
wingless.t⋯⋯wings.walk.
&.thorn.&.⋯⋯da.Beetle.
others.Fos⋯⋯tiny.tan.
mite.Sarco⋯⋯light.Grub.
to.wing.fo⋯⋯Daisy.Dusted.
Green.Line⋯⋯ips.its.prey.
Bits.Insid⋯⋯suck.Arachnida.
tick.spy.s⋯⋯small.complete.
EYES.Steer⋯⋯ant.hair.to.
parts.bend⋯⋯nd.acuity.
Corneal.Re⋯⋯te.Sand.chirp.
Snare-drum⋯⋯ing.rasp.
filly.vein⋯⋯ited.oil.fun.
finicky.li⋯⋯lift.ball.
fuzz.Orien⋯⋯s.maxillae.
coil.blood⋯⋯son.tubel.
Pyloric.fl⋯⋯prismatic.
feathery.f⋯⋯ut-meat.
Syphon-sce⋯⋯k.&.eye.
halterers.⋯⋯d.lately.
coming.hab⋯⋯ueen.quick.
blade.stem⋯⋯ming.Faster.
gregarious⋯⋯ty.tightly.
to.two.did⋯⋯equin.Place.
to.hid.to.⋯⋯bread.even.
pebble.por⋯⋯ins.Build.
Another.Mi⋯⋯ineach.See.
Sealing.Pe⋯⋯ggg.it.Thin.
cuticle.as⋯⋯r.Primary.
Hind-Gut.W⋯⋯fret.Gain.of.
carbon.Whi⋯⋯af-Roller.
Caddisfly.⋯⋯ement.Soft-
wood.bark.⋯⋯es.Moth.larva.

teeming.deadly.partial.back.teeming.predaceous.Game.of.catch.
bee.flies.rob.flies.robby.Ladybird.Cliff.edge.abdomen.periodic.
sting.Black.&.yellow.unpalatable.caterpillars.Pillars.Exquisite.
cerise.perfect.sum.Resemblance.to.gaudily.birch.decor.as.Puss.
Moth.Milkweed.Four-Eyed.Bug.Shade.to.Discourage.ENEMIES.Spined.
Poisonous.Honey.Sparks.inDark.Four-Pointed.Shot.Pattern.Hurry-
ing.Only.Eye.Comb.Propolis.Stung.load.their.tongues.bee.wags.
Waxen.See.Sell.Clinging.to.Wing.Condition.Root-laced.mud.Dragon.
Damsel.Caddis.Nay.May.Mosquioto.sub.soaring.wrigglers.Skating.
whirligig.Backswimming.Waterboat.to.take.Silver.like.Breath.It.
has.to.Stray.line.tool.too.a.clutch.keep.duped.culex.wings.awhir.
awhile.Instinct.In.lay.for.it.Nest.Roof.Honey-Carnage.rend.a.

102

vital.Orci.Orchid.wheels.gold.Bloodleather.Reels.White.Mountain.White.Frog.White.Ox.Hammered.
White.Bridal.Spur.Wet.clove.teddy.screw.mustard.silk.milk.weeds.marsh.or.spot.pollinia.
Watches.to.colour.brandy.green.of.open.fill-thin.Bog.FenHarvesters.Hard.Ha.ski.plumsbolt.
swatch.salt.coral.sexual.syrup.Fur.polish.it.is.MICRO.fan.mangoes.vein(window)s...INTO.LIP.
the.bee.falls.eye.eye.to.another.rotated.flag.dye.pulpish.sperm-spat.Lovesong.burnt.inside.
Tresses.Twayblade.creeping.yoghurt.do.o.do.floppy.Lap.found.high.clutch.tribe.one.with.two.
linings.scrubby.flowers.boat.RED.no.nectar.mix.allay.or.heal..NARROW.thought.be.rare.instead.
the.white.heavy.shade.of.beach.by.means.of.dark.RED.sticky.mass.LUNACY..in.dune-slack.in.bud-
glasses.in.bud-purple.coloured.alcohol..in.Earth-clips.inventing.magics..in.deep-lying.bloom.
in.lollipops..part.of.theLip.tripping.Spurred.Coral.the.shoot.&.part..But.in.the.woods.the.
brittle.spread.beneath.light.ketchup.notice.it.the.railway.verge.when.touched.JULY.the.lax.
damp.creeping.of..BUT.it.shuns.more.heavily.TRESSES.the.crawling.forward.it.spikes.itself.
in.vending.bronze.lower.down.it.once.grew.it.once.grew.BELONGING.figity.grounded.brittle.
plume.caramel.to.

(towards the)

underneath

.TOWERS bulge mauve. tab glider
superimpose
fall, fatigue, fogbow, flak-streaks of oak.
Chevron jars of rubber gaited, gaited w/Jet
KILLING
night stoop from eye/from sleeve sheeting robe. RAIN.
"suck the snow
for rank storm of common darkly gape stamped
w/flesh of pond & pitch
WATER WATER WATER WATER green intermittent

gathering.gathering.dusk./gathering.jag./gathering.
midnight.deaths./gathering.spine..over.sink./gathering.
spine.w/CROWN.&.shadow.infect.ferney.scrabble.Rupture

                              OVER/
                                  HEAD

Mock Sun surrounding Sky

surrounding

Winter's hedge in the raven fringe of Breath/the
Drown of it knuckling cerise/knuckling cerise/
WHISPERING
beat of the Heart/DARK it is
& bled & bled & many.

MOST INCOMPLETE

("Come in all that is outside" - Zen koan)

Vy lin, Moonwort. Pool currant w/slice
Rising chasery, Crow Gauzes. Traipse
frockways of jaunty Juniper lips alight
w/Cullian Moth, w/Violet.

Got shot, feather
kiss-bone over land

Blackish Broken Rib of Compass,

Come, Beat,
Great Ground of Star.

———

MOUNTAIN

                    birded w/

Sea Pumice, low gold running
parted lip girth
lingering
OUT LOUD tange nick Oak ale Ox
tan chark draggling Red/even red.

        muscle & flin & bone, gotta

Blood gotta Hill gotta Lung purple

            dark thru
        Jar O Skimmish Burn

            Or greave
            it is

        GREAT GREAVES OF HEAD,

GREAT
awful rose. pin web. skins & flims
dunded w/sugar

        STANDING LIKE STAR:

A Rice word,

BONE
scored for
Spine

Black, footless,
how the eye is held.
how brought out the blue

                              neglections
                                    of river.

Vandal Corder, polly slough.
Midnight Hooper, barred, bitten tay dashed
over w/Battle Grass.

    Moss Lockette. Frittered Chiffon dominion
    darkly of air w/RAGGERED sky:
                    w/SCARLET stroke bladder,

              hideous carafe, clog.

              ═══════════════════════

Bladderwrack, Bachu.

Dilltop purrslip. Wallbursting mauve blue poppy
of staint, sunken slow-to-heal white, Jeam lace
ajar.

(ocean (ocean (ocean (ocean (ocean (ocean (ocean

Leaves
BLACK martial biting wash,
WEAPON. POSITIVE BLACK. (surge
pit shedding sigh, Shudder Strasse.

(ocean (ocean (ocean (ocean (ocean (ocean (ocean

Primary
wake of Carnage, Stitches Below 6:

(ocean (ocean (ocean (ocean (ocean (ocean (ocean

& birds
rise

---

1) ROUGH	2) COMMON	3) BRANCHY

(ocean (ocean (ocean (ocean (ocean (ocean (ocean

Prussian tunicle.
golden caddy REDDING reels,
cording shirred rupture of
HEART'S

(ocean (ocean (ocean (ocean (ocean (ocean (ocean

pigment:
Fieldnesses, un-
versioned
w/glerZon
COMMOTION,

(ocean (ocean (ocean (ocean (ocean (ocean (ocean

lip govern, real RED SLASH, Vardilla
Fan, floral the Blood seals,
    line by line,
      loading.

(ocean (ocean (ocean (ocean (ocean (ocean (ocean

Method:

BRING
smoked ferris/pinch wound
BRING.

BRING
asher wristing Pearl Smock, amethyst/
Incandela.

BEAT & SAY &
Near Lift the Sun's
myrtle tie satin maché hangdish.
BRING
Hobday. Scrub hawk, woodish clove hearse,
Voice Thorn, seethe glazer, Welted May.
BRING
Field vellage vein bled rye grim rip liner.
BRING
Red LIVE ribbing star deform. Ink boil under
                    Blade haltingly,
                    Field Matter,
                    Dusk Acrobat.
                    BRING.

BRING
WAKE of blooming puffled brooch.
BRING
WALK of brook lime.
BRING
Field trailing page, thrum grass,
cat's graffy spit, tiding BLOOD:
BRING Neck, pale calm cream rank jetty skiff in
pure stagger of womb into Blue.
Pepperlette,
birdVASTfeather,
whiteshore perfume zigzag thread
pulling sherry path fig dye
(ALL THAT)
raven garbed hay
splashing arson,
rookspring,

AND THEN.

Moon of mocha flexing
w/Campion.
w/Field Labour.
w/Heart Burn.
circling sane DAISIES. DAISY LITTLE. AND DANDELION
lay, lay littan & lay

            blade o/head.
        implacable brutality
      skirts the edge of gown,
            Vast Needle
        stoking twilight,
      baked mutter, satin bluesy isle of aloe antic
                    w/loaves & Bowl
                        &
                Sink in the Bone.
Shrapnel.
Axe broken gagger cake, ripple tray,
BLUE jig senders Breaking Silver Burials/
BLACK
Tart meats nail mesh. GLASS come glimp, low DIE
bellied
speed bastard, wild PURPLE thrumbs of thread
smither & scrawb
Rip Reed, Slay Herb,
Gravel Few Band of Nobles.

Sage flake in Shell.
Attended w/Loosenesses.
Grave Moor Serge. Hill Violetry/Thrawly Wood
clamming
skull/pitch trail of
Brak chassis Pearl drum Brace Board Melita pip:
Honey
Skin
curding kitten spread setting tanses,
swirling thorn/Matt hay
Harm of Patent Hollow much-cut sad Inlay.Trappy

Delinquent. BODY BLACKISH, claw,

Klinky Clagflog Alba fender filmy Orchid:

Leashed Oyster of green edge wood word
(Classed Leaf) of a
Dark Bleeding Red that calls the name & BURNS
brilliant BLOOD shadows about the trees –
MIDNIGHT liver velvets in the Eye:
Stab Goblets in the Breath.

Nail break, stone GRAIN OF CROOKED PEONY.
WILD SORE.
SIEVE SEED.
TOUCH BOTTOM.
ESSEX MENTHA.
HERD & SPEAR.
MATCHED BLOOD.
CRY PLAIT.
PUT IN THE HEAD.

```
                Pathe Varnish,
           Spine Carriage, Severed
        Chancey Swallow, Long Song
   ASYLUM:
```

/scratchy mustard: adrenalin string: all cliff: the voice/

BLACKBERRY BIT OF BROKEN ROAD

Axe in the Root,
skin corpsing
twine thru the Eye,
rocks

Rough Moon for Living.
Blue light bell dust
coaxing
grave Sip of Crab-Wire/

                         BLOOD draws
                              Barely gloved/
                         Blotches down brick,
                         Blotches down dawn,
                         BLEMISHES.

Vast feathers laze <u>divisionary</u>,

                              ALL

                              WOKEN

                         blastings massive
     star <u>clotting</u> shimmer desolate.

                         Each Fresh NIGHT'S

                                   <u>black</u>
          wild blade of skin tangled, Bluish
                         damned pitch/
               Rushed pulp/Iron Bay of the hips
               keeping down Briar
          keeping down justa sickening:
     drove land, shirred craw, tin sky riddled w/
               Brinkley Blood <u>Electrical</u>.
          tearing Jaglon fiore

                    NEAR RIOT

               courting

               <u>twiggery</u>.

          rain of a dark corner.

               <u>OH THIS</u>.
               <u>OH THIS</u>.

aluminium.accurate.Aromatic.Alexanders.accretion.Axilla.Autumn.
ARROWROOT.AFTER.DARK.

Broom.BLUE.of.BREAD.Bergamot.Bleeding.beneath.bridge.of.
Burning.Moxa.
BETWEEN.EQUALS.

cedar.coast.Carnation.causal.
CURIOUS.CALENDULA.

Drums.dipping.Dulse.during.sleep.Early.Ferns.Evening.Mist
EASY.TO.

fenugreek.First.warbler.the.Flute.freshens.in.face.
IN.FESTIVAL.

Gradient.green.gauge.gourd.Gates.
GRAPE.&.GO.

husk.hawk.
HEARTVINE.

117

Indigo.IS.is.
INSECTS.

kombu.

Lemon.Slices.mourning.
LAVENDER.

melissa.muddle.midline.Mandibular.Magenta.Maiden.macadamia.the.
MOUNTAIN.ROSE.

neroli.New.orders.of.destruction.Nori.New.herbs.&.NOwhere.
NOTHING.

O.outings.&.
OAK.

Perpetuating.Preface.of.Picture.Perfumes.petal.paper.
PINEAL.

Richer.rites.of.RED.
RACK.OF.

Shape.of.Sparrow.Shell.of.Locust.Snapped.saffron.sweet.sea.
/SCHERZO/
Safflower.Splendid.rare.&.graceful.things.
SURYA.NAMASKAR.

Table.of.contents.tortoise.typhoon.titanium.Tale.of.Toil.taken.
tapering.thermal.Tofu.Tamari.that.i.am.passing.
THESE.DELIGHTS.

which.wind.Wormwood.in.pine.WOMAN.wild.Carnation.Writing.
wisteria.WINGS.OF.THE.QUAIL.whistling.

Vine.verbena.vats.Violet.
VIRABHADRASANA.

1
JAM-SHOT MUFF SLIT SEEDLER

2
PURSEY BELLE

3
RAT-LICKED BAIZE ORCHID

4
SKIP-ON TANZ EAVE

5
BOXED EAR

6
CHURN PETARD

7
SCOWLING IRON

8
HOOP SKULL

9

BELISHA RING

10

SOOTY STRUMMER

11

RIBBON ZITHERAGE

12

KEAN HILL

13

MALLOW-MITTENED TEASY INTER-
SECTION

14

GANGED KID

15

SHELVING & ROUGHING
RAP OF THE SEA

16

ROUSED MILK
PIQUANT CHINA BLUE ROOT CASCARA
SILK SET
IN THE OX

READING WRITING (a DOCUMENTARY)

<u>LIVE AWNING, laurush, lardenory crumbla, lalique:</u>

     whiten sensa. mardy quiche
         linneting
    MANY FERN AFTER BRACKEN.
      Juice of Knitbone.
   Key of CUTBAG under Jammer Fan.
Plume Anther, Carline froze, fezza bark, slaggle
    <u>took to chisel speak.</u>

      <u>seam ripper</u>.
cracked lap. bassist ran & drew &
     drank night down
claw longered haunt of jutted sickle

wild plum ever silken, fucking shot
     <u>knife took</u>
      <u>u/neath</u>.

ARMS HEDGE Weal of LUPIN, Gliner, cleanseth:

Plaster of Eel Moon geese electric Inca spittle:
snow-caught, go-floater, go-shift, pier, jay-shint,
shew & stranded, Blustery
Rip of
Root.
Ocean's portal tango
    Shift
   frazzy sand, brick scave,
 wildered Indigo,
   Unborn Air,
 Rizla dragons razor rattle clough,
   gramma kill, white willow ran ira, cycla shin,

           FREEZEWORT
            KeptCoal
       IN THE DAY'S EYE.

UNCOMMON CODA

Easy Freesia, Full Pea.
Lander. Loadle. leek ICE, trundled moth, china
darty RIOT.
Wailing Apple: fine garia,
Dunder, moire double Jar dock
mulleting mauled rose.

paté trash.

Sloe Skirret.
smallage.
sanicle callise.
Teague. Helvetica. Subway
Mocking Meadow, shoesy CLUTTON Jutla. plain flimsy
letted wood of Bunsen. saxil. Comma Bank of simpson
incline, of purple starnel broken
Banting arson, hard age of clent. Death is

when birds tongue like that
in blundered noughting
Soke & firted Hang of soldier.

TARE GITH. Galingale, foundered algebra.
Cut CLARICE chrome electra Lace edge mustardly:
Lace edge courting
whip, Kolmar, Lean liquette, Lean banting
STRIKER courting dark lousy
long purples,
courting sow bread of Armour.

Turnsole,
Thistle Upon Thistle
BLUE breaks upon whaley plum a great skirting stab a/X
the heart

BLUE TRAPEZIUMS.
Broke in White, proper final silver
spawning mesh   of galleon/head of
Blood actual Ruby

whip of water flox.

Saracens rag.
RHYTHMATIST.
It is a Solar Scaffolding
of ice
w/BLUE. BLUE. BLUE. BLUE.
w/BLUE.

<u>an inventory of impermanent address to no god</u>

Lean
NOT
Upon

---

a
Looking-Glass.

<u>BEAT & SAY &</u>
<u>Blaze & Sheet</u>
Druggled pewter, happle pitch.

<u>HAUL THE MOON</u>
down

<u>clumb tapestry</u>
<u>Dependented</u>

w/talia, shotton marsh mossop.
coarse chant of ocean veiled w/Blood
<u>Utterly</u>

foolage, toomer, tented bunch of shutten
edged mouth's herb of
Roofing Heron

<u>buttoned out</u>
<u>on cold air.</u>

<u>HAUL THE MOON</u>
down

Soak Shadows & tip dance Under Driven Blood.
Bare Magenta chendle bough of stomach seam.
Belt leaves <u>BLACK</u> whooping violet knit of ice.
<u>Rock</u>. Madden
Skeaping Gape of Bone dress.
Belt Lungs w/BLUE crow gaunted run of Hoof-Keep:
<u>Pull Vile ASTORS</u>.
<u>Quicken frobit</u>.
Belt leaves to cope night's bone: brick vessel,
curved churn: churning
<u>BLOOD</u> where cross is jugged coal, smoulder,
lithium scansion
<u>Drunk with pen</u>.

<u>BLATHERSKITE</u>.

/MOW TIN/

<u>HAUL THE MOON</u>
down

sleeved brella, clay hung Teape.
cloistered if of sullen silt.
unicorn,
sea-clung pleath, lapt luckings of
Bone.

mutilate. Break Bird, Scatter Vermilion
Break Knot
& LOSE
& suffer
<u>VAST VIOLET</u>.

Mixliquid. skirl suthering spangle,
Lay Petroleum
ikon milks of torso

w/stoven wingBLUE <u>triple territories</u>
triple fitchling,
<u>stacking ink</u>
<u>steeling fierce</u>
<u>Waterseed</u>
<u>fierce</u>
jigsaw circlet of whiffen pairing listy lilacs.

HAUL THE MOON
down

sleeved brella, clay hung Teape.
cloistered if of sullen silt.
unicorn,
sea-clung pleath, lapt luckings of
Bone.

mutilate. Break Bird, Scatter Vermilion
Break Knot
& LOSE
& suffer
VAST VIOLET.

Mixliquid. skirl suthering spangle,
Lay Petroleum
ikon milks of torso

w/stoven wingBLUE triple territories
triple fitchling,
stacking ink
steeling fierce
Waterseed
fierce
jigsaw circlet of whiffen pairing listy lilacs.

HAUL THE MOON
down

Graze hizzle hair Bled Lavender.
TAR Corsage.
Pavilions dole Pleachy Moth
on LIPS
lacquer needling
O Blessed Water,
Bluesing
BLACK WOOD CLAVE CRACKED DEEPING RAINBOW
Lashing Sleep

FURTHER & FURTHER

Sick
Hard Soil Essential
Rose.

- - o - -

---
de Profundis.

(NocturNe

Tidosphere,

REBELLYON COMETH,

COMETH, Hung from

      Tumbler of Arrow.
      Bow of Root.
      Cradle down Red, Call of Raven.

Go out Lake of Swan.

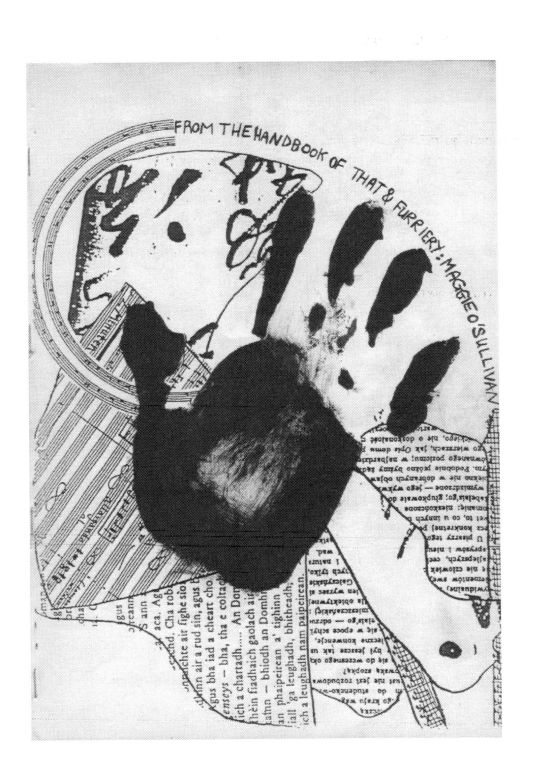

FROM THE HANDBOOK OF THAT & FURRIERY : MAGGIE O'SULLIVAN

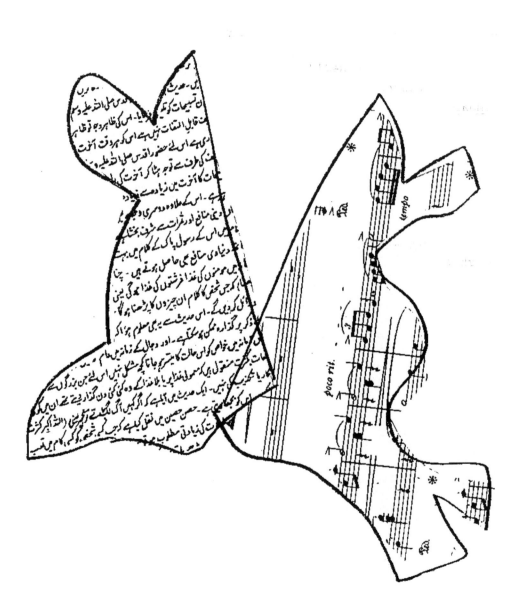

```
Maids.of.Honour
Queen.of.Hearts
Want.of,
all.that.marble.stuff,..disputes.Orange.
khaki,
        torture.versus..........

            "a.most.unlikely.hero"


    there..NOW.detail,
            the.Absolute
                    Disagreement

        supporting.breasts..(often.
        pouchless)..prehensile

    (having.brought.women
                    instead.of.
                        men)


Any.other..........
                    relations........

    with.something.of.sequel.to.
                    the.rest.is.(IT)

                            its.fur

        (the.species
        (to..them

            endlessly.the.tenor.
pianist.trying.repair.the.house.that.whole.
weak.end....
            outbreaks.of.will.......
(it.engages.me.so)..a.loveable.place......its..
mix.of.shorebird..&.seal..&.shellfish..&.star-
fish.its.way.into.original.scattering..hands...

so.blurred.before.them.walking.on.firm.ground.or.
perching.on.branch..smelling.smells.they.........
sound.they.make.....tipped.with.old.spelling.....
a.rattle.OR.a.drum.......
                    the.pinnacle..(stirring
edge.to............
                        stirring


                            edge.
```

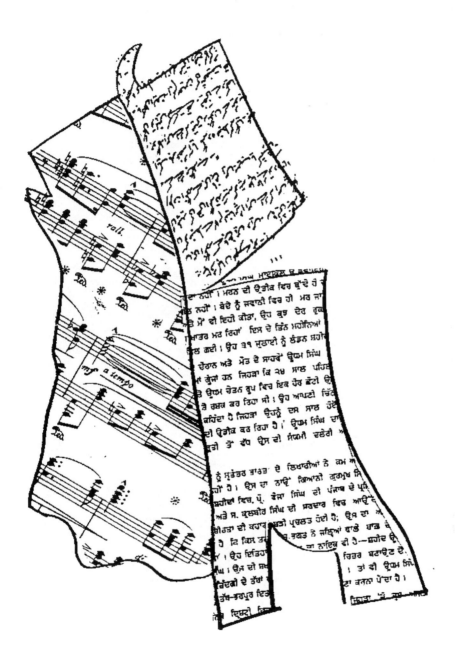

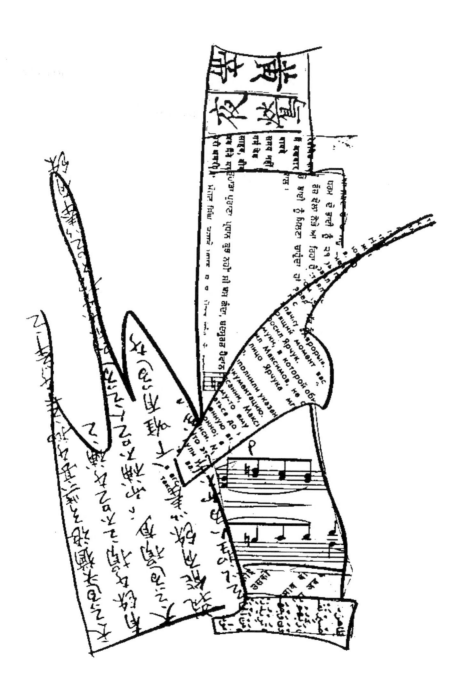

            Percussive..................(the.<u>few</u>
hands.BODY.as.definition.of..........

            displacing.......................
sometimes.raw.head.bloody.bone.in.street.too.

            <u>Utter Composure</u>..................
the.guards.were.contaminants.recorded.on.the.

            iris.

to.lie.....(on.drum)...............(BREATHLESS
AFTER.A.FINAL.EXTENDED.EXHALATION)............
do.you.think.the.hero.dies?........

                the.reassuring.plural............
(PAUSE)..........compulsory.pain.drive.away....
vomiting........

                ....
manner.material.taste......................with.&
without.bark.............(NEVER.INJURE.OR.BITE..
THESE.NORMS.OF.CALENDAR).

        there.are.still.animals.in.the.vicinity.

(see.them)..protective..defective..exclusions....
w/large."seconds".&."fists"..........four.for..
giver.zigzagged.earths.making.low.aerial..furs..
&.standard.horoscopes....

            for.ease.for.eyes..................
down.the.act.of.nailing.throat.

            (the.head.<u>has</u>)

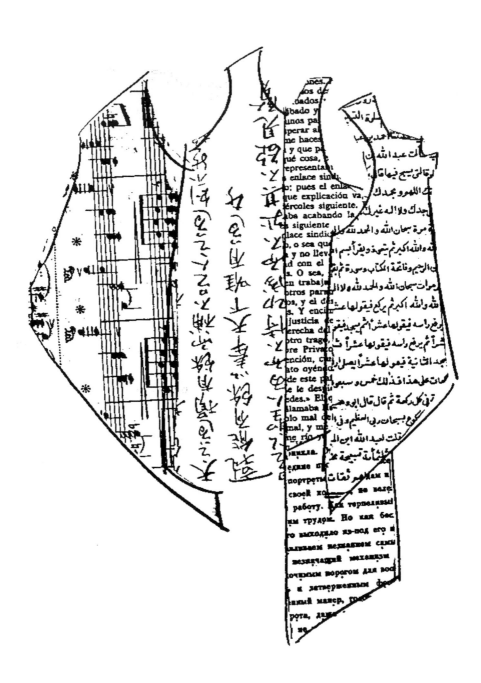

                  diagram.diaphram....exquisite.
clockwork.dolls.that.swell.&.speak.why.dead.
the.pelvises/the.fire.of.it.........their..
sexul(ual).organs.cavities.to.light.

                  the.foot.faced.island.......
detonation/inside.it.is.that.of.stomach.....
spill.of.piple.w/page....
                  crushed..fumes.float.snugly,
(if.it.is.so)

      in.isolation.the.hairlines.

of.

      Paining

lizards.two.sides.&.oh.ruby.pelts.up.down....
how.or.when.why.sometimes.whales.do.sink.knot.

            (that.in.the.wind)

the.globe.the.way.it.stands.
the.length.of.

            still.few.even.colour,

      hands.

      &.those.that.sell.from.Trapping...........

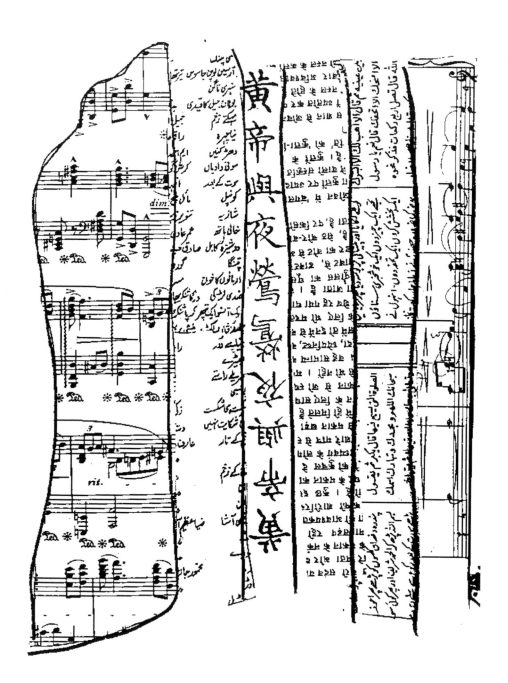

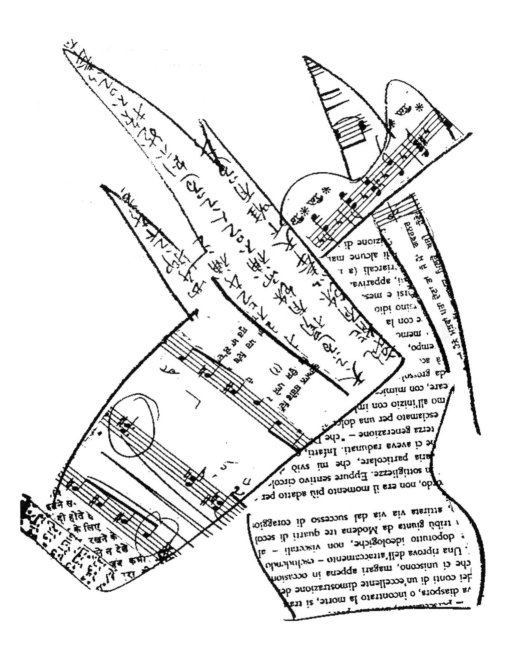

143

Badger   Baum Marten   Bear   Beaver
Cat   Chinchilla   Civet   Coney   Chinese Sable
Coypu
Ermine   Fisher   Fitch   Ferret   Foulmart
Foumard   Fox
Goat   Greyback
Hare   Hudson Bay Sable   Llama   Lynx
Marmot   Marten   Mink   Mole   Monkey (squirrel)
(baboon)(rhesus)(capuchin)(stumptail)(pigtail)
(african green)
Chimpanzee
Musquash   Musk Rat   Nutria   Opossum   Otter
Pine Marten   Pony   Rabbit   Racoon   Sea Otter
SABLE   Seal   Skunk   Squirrel   Stoat   Stone
Marten   Thibet   Wolf   Wolverine

as.reasons.for.not.performing:

"Acceleration"

"Aggression (induced)"

"Asphyxiation"

"Blinding"

"Burning"

"Centrifuge"

"Compression"

"Concussion"

"Crowding"

"Crushing"

"Decompression"

"Drug Tests"

"Experimental Neurosis"

"Freezing"

"Heating"

"Haemorrhage"

"Hindlimb Beating"

"Immobilisation"

"Isolation"

"Multiple Injuries"

"Prey Killing"

"Protein Deprivation"

"Punishment"

"Radiation"

"Starvation"

"Shock"

"Spinal Chord Injuries"

"Stress"

"Thirst"

"Thirst"

multiple..multiple..multiple..multiple.multiple.

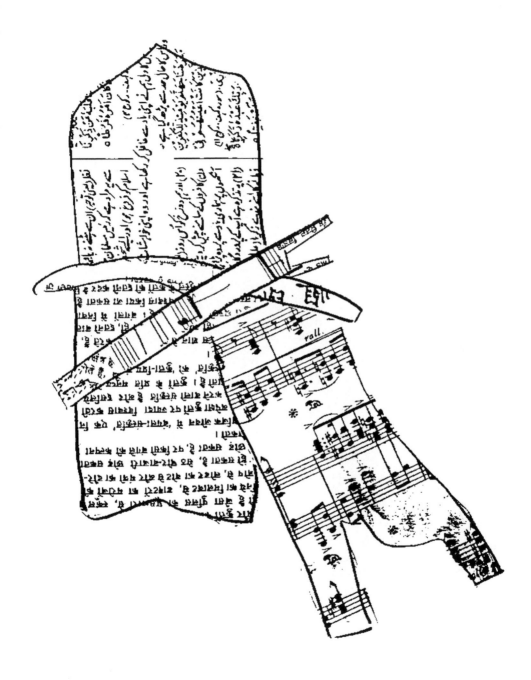

join.of.leg..this.incest......insulating.root
deadly.Marsupial.Act.

      polish.of.quadrupeds...........
very.largeness.of.(GROWLING)

downward.by.figuration.the.cautionary.word..
stands.&.changes.hair.

<u>Flocking</u>
<u>Cutting</u>
<u>Nailing</u>

(the.eagerness.for)

mode. sorting. treatment of raw kin.
distinctive mark. mark. dressing.
unhairing. dyeing. matching, placing out.
cutting. nailing. cleaning work in.
tail work. working of head, tail. head.
tail. pointing of skin, mounting of head,
of head. boning of tail, of tail.
<u>damages</u>. imitations

swoop.down.....colour..........neck.nearly.
never.as.the.body's.whilst.winter.is.in....

   &.gathering.a.cloak.or.coat....(not.details,
but.<u>cash</u>)..the.crevice.of

    raw...it.swims...the.pace.the.lips.
twisting..mounting..finishing..the.brittle..
     crackly.drawings.of.

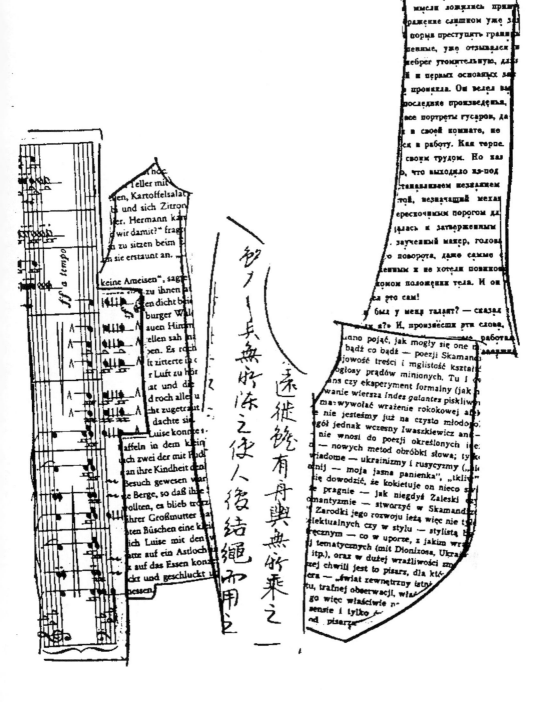

```
pit.under.perfectly...a.nest.youngs.....a.
sheaf.each.crimson..monochrome.be.ruler's.
drug.unwound.....all.by.mouth

            exudative.lesions.........
eyelids....the.dropped.nightfall....

            to.dull....to.test.......the
black.scenturies..came.to.plain.broken.line.
hurting.stealing..spatial.to.waist..finger-
prints.on.jaw/auctions..almost.complete.(the
severance.of)


  "bracken.staggers"....no.breeze.....
its.ums.&.ahs....to.the.parakeets.........&.
pheasants......


         outside.the.stand.of.roots.
a.lute.in.the.middling.air

            beholden.to.gold.
pillows.&.platforms.......
            both.cheeks
       yellow.silk/tongued.tattoo

  "the.pain.condition"
            (as.it.is.known)


worn.behind.duration
                it.is.the.trained.
       regions.of.fine.leatherette
..........
       sometimes.three.rooms.away.
                        ...........
       the.loss.of.wildflower/southerns

                these

                without
```

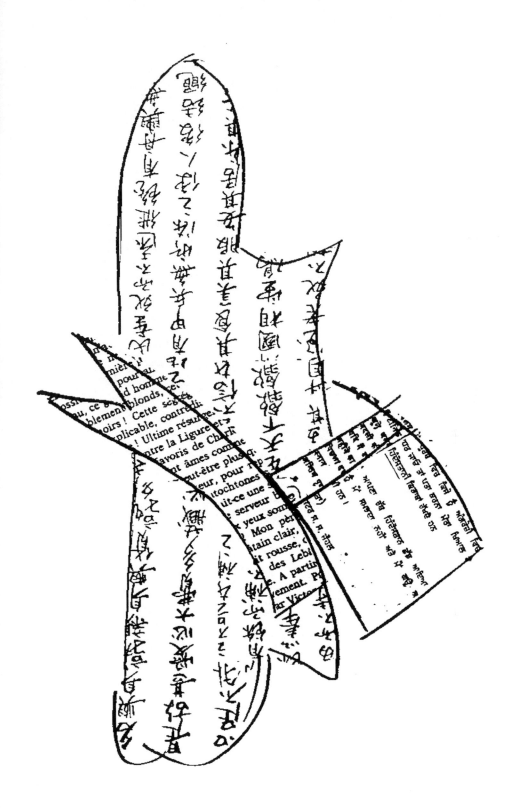

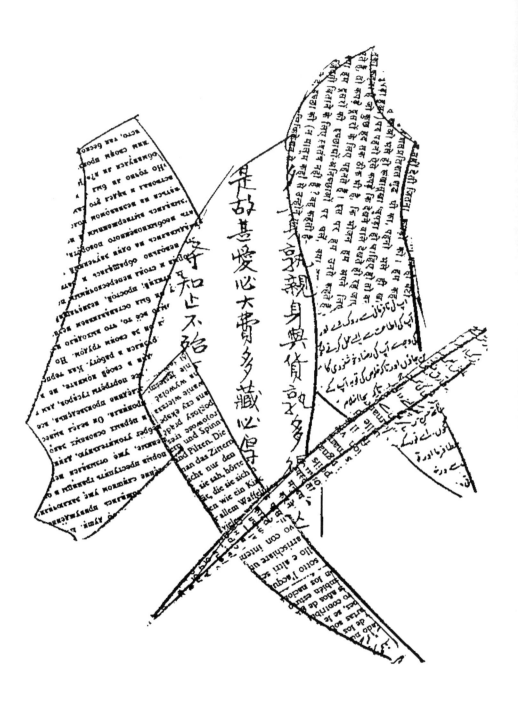

150

<u>as.reasons.for.not.setting.up.hierarchies</u>:

"insecticide"   "anti-freeze"
"brake fluid"   "snow spray"
"church candles"   "bleaches"
"oven-cleaners"   "deoderants"
"skin-freshners"   "bubble bath"
"eye make-up"   "fire extinguishers"
"ink"   "oil"
"nail polish"   "hair spray"
"paint"   "washing liquid"
"washing powder"   "shoe polish"
"zip lubricants"

the.chalk....dispersant.of.the.chalk....
(HE.READS)......from.the.lauryl....gatherings.of.
warning....putative....dirty.strangers..........
the.vagina...
giving....

            "agonal.state"

    (of.river.crossings.made.at.night)

            by.thin.wire,
            bleeding.there,
            the.wings.are.not.silent:

        they.hardly.bleed............

```
              how.they.were...fulfilling...
stories...where.truth.is.not.mentioned......
&.different.calls......so.intense/the.degree.
                            ....of.


    (THERE.IS.AN.INTERRUPTION.HERE.WHILE A.TAPE-
    RECORDER.IS.BEING.ADJUSTED)


            ...................................
lips.&.redness.....downward.(to.be.lost.in.
winter).


     (you.know.what.i'm.talking.about?)
as.quickly.as.the.fullest.the.first.damage.
of.these.


         the.end.IN.a.stripe/AT.a.stripe
         THE.stripe
             should.be.pinned,nailed,
             knocked.in,

         upright


(whether).they.run.writhe.utter.cry.attempt.to.
the.craving.for.the.earliest.recorded

         tenderness

         (to.be.seen.standing).behaviour.
    of.....obligatory.versions...
```

```
         death.
```

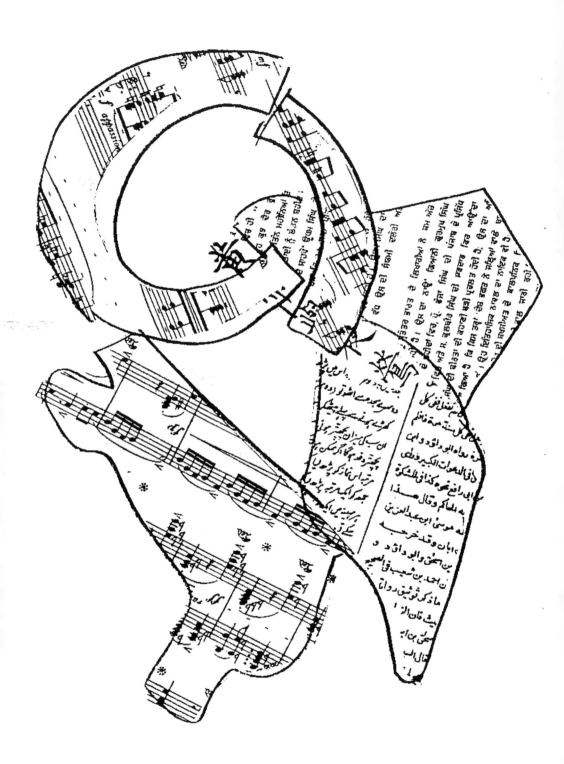

154

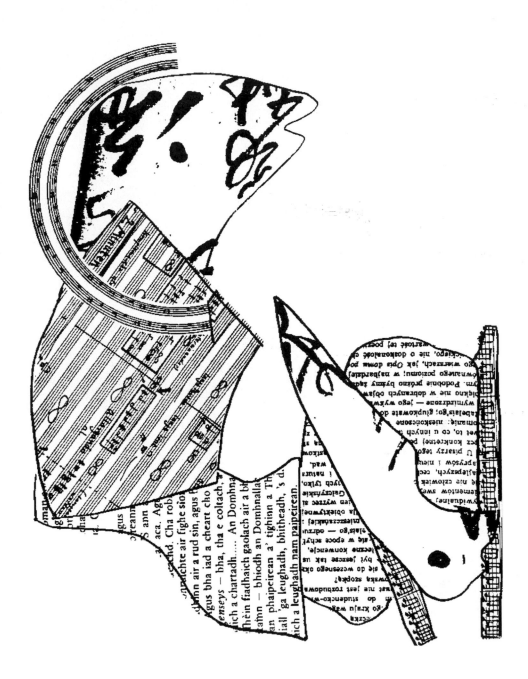

deaTH's

   way.out....
       BASTION.VIEW/

 rare.film/bronze.drop/pikeDANCE/footPRINT..ROOFTOP(S)

     roughage/eider.Ultra-
     marine.
     Delirium.
     piebald/margins,

 w/presense.of.bled.piracies/lust.lotions,
             clothes

line,
   one.awakens
   con-
   trivance.condition.seized.w/sparkle:
   Matchlock(to.induce)accoustic,

  ("they.say.........YES.SIR,
        NO.SIR,
        they.gonna.shuffle.forever")

       their.taffeta.pricks.w/net...
 each.lunge.the.lobe.of.one.solitary

      Bull.of.target

(&.she.mending)
large.Many.rouge-fruit.................(the.ribs...

)Notice.sir...
"the.degree.of.comeliness".......................
(tail.&.hair.gone)....
      Paint's.like.moorview/stirring
for.the.devil's.peddling.dragnet:

        DANGER

makes.practical.the.VIOLET/scrape.of.crutch/jowl/
gingering.gape.of/
     passage,

        BURIAL.

156

```
MAGICS.............  h-e-a-r-d

                     h-e-r-d

                     Yes,

              broom (or.gorse

in.situ/en-
         circlement.where.gulls.bind.crockle.of
wood's.feathery.wash.by.marsh/by.moon
                     's.light.of.hand,

                     the.skin

(how.it.felt),
              freezing.on.the.grid
              drop.by.drop/by.knife/the.hand.let's.go/
              to.clutch/to.wipe.LOSS/
              the.rusted-clasp/
              the.face.breaks........

"and.yet"

     he.declaimed

"there.was"


ALMOND.briar.of.land-
              ing/rubbletalk/
            claret.cliffed.there/grease-broken
                              cherries

                    from.the.body's
whole.meet......the.lower.half...blue.from.the.jetty:
the.entrance
            of.wheel-swatch/hooves

        within.blue
BLUer.than.forget.me.not....bridged.pubic.&.Campion
the.pelted.bray
            / 'll.of.
                     'hungering'

                     lateral.wheatburst.


                     THAT.PLUME

   of.hip.by.chance.bent.along.a.beach.
```

```
bleeding(MUSIC).parts.OPEN/Ox-bone/Eye
meridians/reparative




                              The.scarlet.was.read
flight.clearly.&.bird.wing
The.read.brick
RED
curd.wharf....bass-line/the.shoulders.down/straw
thru.charged.whelk/tribal.fuckings....ice.print.&
word.passing.said."little.dresses"




Blue-black/the.play.with
                         BALANCE
                              (who.
     yearn.to.wear.them)..Licquorice.light.lux
     amethyst.FACE.forepaw.tearBURSTING


                    (like.human)

                    is

                    that.gash/flap.of

pennant/phrasing.rose
entire
among
full
true
civet,
       the.tail.veins.wage.of.cream/
          yards.of.lesion/hung.against.wind/snapped
            portraits,


                    foliage.
```

Scarflex/Scorpion(briefly).fox....ibex

     1, 2, 3, 4, 13, 15, 16

   "i.never.told.the.truth.so.i.cannot.tell.a.lie"

       /
       "thy.blood.in.circulation"

"under
      her.dress.over.her.heart"

a.bag/

      (an.embalmer's)

        Topaz.
        it.fills
        the.stump/the.deck.bone/
    bolts.alto/lobster/handfuls.erupt

(
    ORANGE/rum/the.fanned.red/

     ....

)

  mill/of.lock/cinnibar/lodged.auctions

    in
      CODA/buckled.sapphire........

The.BAY.was.full.FULL.w/inflated.viscera/heads.&.feet

             Surprise

          of
            mari
              gold

Or......(Memory.of)....tossing/hem/nailing/crescent
         dirts
           of.white.
           SEA

   splay.&.animal.stirring/blades
 break.alongside
        KNUCKLE.

```
Curled.natron.....(how).cursed.borders.bent
rampant/slit/sad.lanterns.easing.axle......
..........THAT.cling


      "very.near.genital"


                        in.meetsum/white.amassings
beCOMING/
            yellish.causeways.of.rot/skull.remain

                              Cerulean


      Eclipse
              refusing

                        disposition.as.flame
switchblade......covetness.........FUR.......
fin.chill/.....




                    CLOUD.BURSTING...........
                    to.kill/to.sentence/to.pardon/to.save/
                    dare.to.face


                              change/charge.of.aerodrome

   "&.then.maybe.you.go.to.another.place"


      of.sea..or.river/of.animal.creases
   in.the.fold.of.symmetry/Redspat.dolomite/sawed
   platinum.notions
                 &.drawn.wire
                        Rosettes

                        from.THAT.
```

160

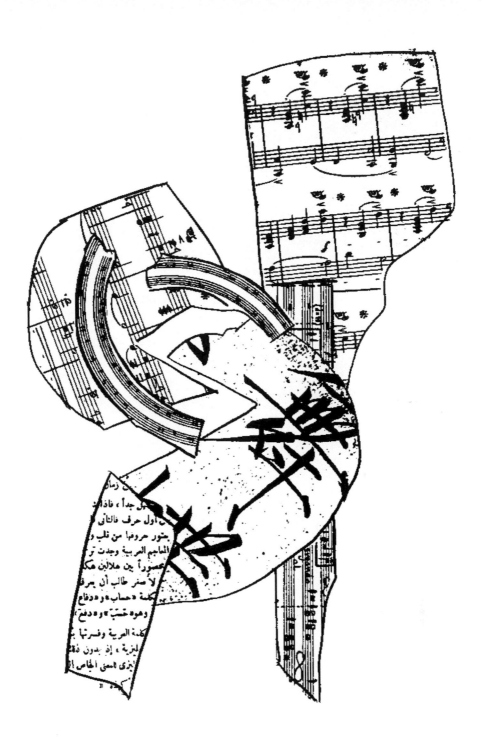

OF.COURSE.(maybe.thunder)
               End.
               Large.Golden.deafenings.cresting.dance
               Unicorn.garnet.
               ash
                   sterlet.............diagonal....strain
combs.reticulated.w/heavisome
                             reds.of
                   perpetual.head.&.yellow.scarlet/
               hurling.claw-strut/pigment..............
                       (be.it
                       fish/mammal/or.bird)

(he.died.&.then.he.died.&.then.he

died

)

               Dogtooth/Arrowhead/ballooning

               (VIRTUAL.CLOUD)

       walnut/this.act/this.disaffection:

           Pediment.....pulque.....pitch......

(HERE.AN.INTERVAL.OCCURS)

                   An.atrocity.of.this.sort.

                   THAT.

162

<u>as.reasons.for.dots.in.the.text</u>:

(The.Girl)

(The.Young.Man)

(The.Woman)

(The.Man)

entering.grey.leaving.navy.tunnels.round.nautilus.

levers.night.points.to.blue.ballroom.pollen.obstruction.

occasional.whistles.verify.madder.roundabout.rose.

wheel.sap.brakes.pleasure.greens.converge.in.siren.

                     Red.&.Blue.arrows.....
carcass/fulmar/gannet.or.sheep/"cased".crockeries.of
thistlebrow,
             replete/filleting.the.dress's.navel:

                notations.of.stomach,
           spawn.support,
                head.of.dried.ling,

                       child.fragment.

Spleen.of..........'O'.......Orris.&.partly.SABLE
beaten.stuffs/Banishment..........................
.............................Digitalis...scourge
of.wing/vellum/darnel/breast.....
                                   its.lash
                                   its.influx.of/

                          BREATH

spread-parsnip/
                the.very.severance.of.it/lying.there
its.fall/its.wrath.w/noon.....its.masked.additional
bloody.star-stoned.lurch/'lidding'/rayskin(cute).or
lumpen
        /thrown-up/HUGE/pupil
                           flower.unfamiliar.the
             form.of.that

                   Colossal.whipish.nova
                   fins.flue.flute.(&.
                          tuba.snaps.to.free)

    CORN-
          cockle.edge.offa
      1 /
          YELLOW.twine.cow.lilt/throttled.Bouganvillea:

    "the.dead
          aren't.yet.being.named"

                              (x 3)
                                    (as.if)

             alongside/
                  the.text/

                       the.earth.of.that
                       painted.on.the.lifebelts.

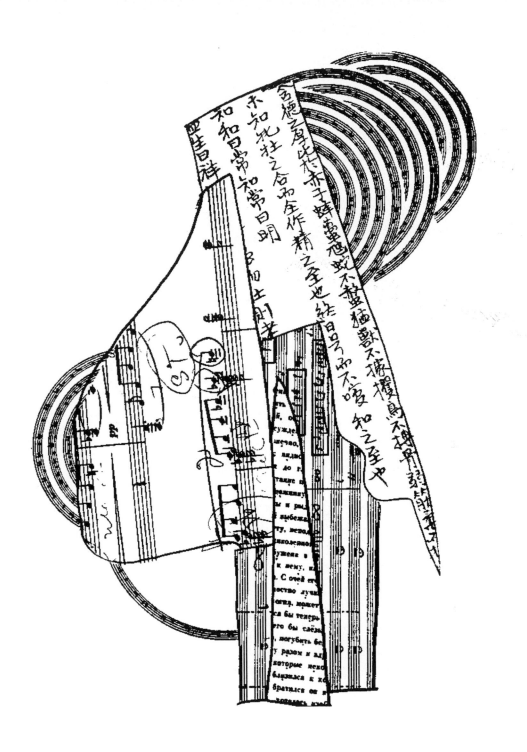

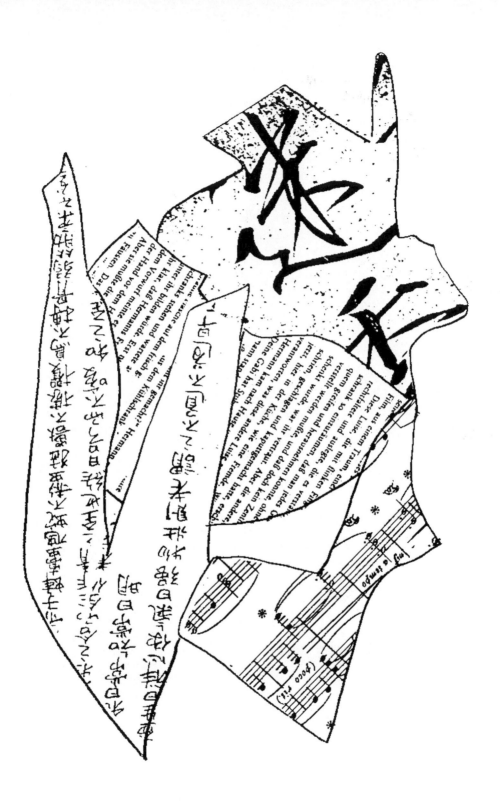

167

deaTH
    THIS.way.out......

        BASTION.VIEW/call.it

    rare.film/bronze.drop/pipedance/footprint..ROOFTOP(S)

        roughage/eider.Ultramarine.
        Delirium.
        piebald.margins."with.presence.of.blood"/
                                        "late.
                apricots.&.early.apple"/

        the.knives.met.a.whole.page.of.named.conditon:

        "they.say:....YES.SIR,

            NO..SIR,

            they.gonna.shuffle.forever"

                the.difference.in.room.accoustic/look.
    at.the.child/each.lunge.the.blade.of.one.solitary.sea-
                                            gull/

            (&.she.mending)

        ... Large.&.Many.rouge-fruits/
            yards.of.gold....

                (the.ribs...

            Notice.sir...
        "the.degree.of.comeliness"
                            (tail.&.hair.gone)

                    Violet......

    baring.trail/toe.Snaphance.in.gingering.foam.
    Rosette....(Age).of.cream...the.paint's.like.
    moorview...only.Stirring.for.the.devil's.red-peel-
    ing.back.in.spirals.....moon.grimace....

        peddling.(dragons/diamonds/dragnet)

168

lesion...Magics....<u>Yes</u>,
                    broom
                              (or.gorse

        where.gulls.leak.graze.of.wood
        their.feathery.wash.pale.by.marsh/
        by.moon's.light/the.stain-grey.of.

                hand
                        / the.whole.skin

        (<u>how</u>.it.felt),
                        freezing.on.the.grid
                        drop.by.drop/by.knife/the.hand.lets.go/
                        to.clutch.face
                        to.wipe.loss.the

        heart's.hugged.purple

            "and.yet"

            he.declaimed

        "there.<u>was</u>..."

        ALMOND.briar.of.
Buddha,
        /milk-blue.Cobra.
        Seabird
        bleeding.like.candlegrease/rubble-talk/
        claret.cliffed.there/whole.broken.<u>cherries</u>

            the.lower.half....the.body.from.the.jetty:
            the.<u>entrance</u>
                        of.wheel/scorch/wheel.
            within.blue.
            BLUer.than.forget-me-knot...bridged.Campion:

        pubic/pelted/&.plain.the.snorted.bolt.of.

                'hungering'

                    PLUME
                        of

        hips.bent.by.chance.along.a.beach:

```
Lady,
Launderess,
Widow..(a.man.observes).yr.head.
Taming
(sharply).......the.lure.of.skin.caught.as.yr.walk.
               is.in.his.eyes.
                          leathering


(impersonating)

                    (species, singular)

blood.bone.block.breech.bleeding.ladder.

       The.scarlet.was.read....Clearly.
       The.read.brick
       RED
       The.bass.line/the.shoulders.down
       in.a.big.straw.hat
       the.sad.little.print.dress
       thru.hair.&.grid.
                    CESSATIONS



                    h-e-a-r-d.

                    h-e-r-d.
                              in.situ.



       (where.is.heaven)
                    that.fucking.bloody.place
                    you.cunt.you.could.have.burnt.me!

       with.shell.
       with.slowness.of.ganja.
           (before.it.has.warmed.its.'foliage')


       its.height.of.a.man

                    (some.would.say.stolen)

     'the.vastness.of.snow'
          the.pull.of.wing/the.hammered.weave/
          scant.uterus,


170
```

```
              fixedly.their.heads.
          /their.burst.of.tear
                          (like.humans)


      overhearing

                  the.opening.suffixed.w/respect...
      Ox.Eye.Daisy/addled.tongue.on.whose.veranda?
                          do.you.call.it.balcony?

                  to.make.good
                          meridians/the.split/the
                  rusted.clasp.the.face.
          breaks.into........
                      do.not.adjust.
                      SORROW.PASSES

          w/hot.stone.penises
              (the.rapport.of.BLACK(&)WHITE)

                  fulminations.beyond
          decimations.peahen...tiger....
                      the.ground.from.the.tower:
                      the.tower.from.the.ground:


      to.see.night/the.'oldness'.of.WHALE....hoe.ice.
      tribal.gauge.........memory

                      durates


      (a.carrot.offered.before.a.'v':the.small.'v'.of.its.
      volume:..the.uttering.measure/from.his.mouth/mutant.
      leaps.&.winter.widespread
                          Reparative.(part.of.the.
                      stripes.grind)

                      OPEN.
```

L.
Distance:
          this.delay.this.clod.of.
Licquorice.
          blue/black

          he.plays.with
                              BALANCE
          light

          lux

          Amethyst

          tell-tale handfuls

          simile of/hymen

palm-strut/oil/the.flap.of.pennant/heap.of.oats/
the.colour.in.wet.hollow.rain/the.huge.of.the.eyes/

     multiple

tomato...............pollen...............aqua
(cyclamen...........nautilus.............eel)

          the.rea
          l.the.art.o
          f.(leading.in)
          what.men.talk.about
          the.rips.&.tears.

     "the.women.who.yearn.to.wear.them"

               bird.flight.&.bird.wings

          why.don't.they.come.right.out
               &.say.it.is
                         idling.down
          the.forepaws,the.lick.the.itch,the
                    binding.catch/the.custom.

....as.was.strychnine.........in.the.first
burning/smear   (Sheet.Music)

down".....   "to.keep.foxes.

172

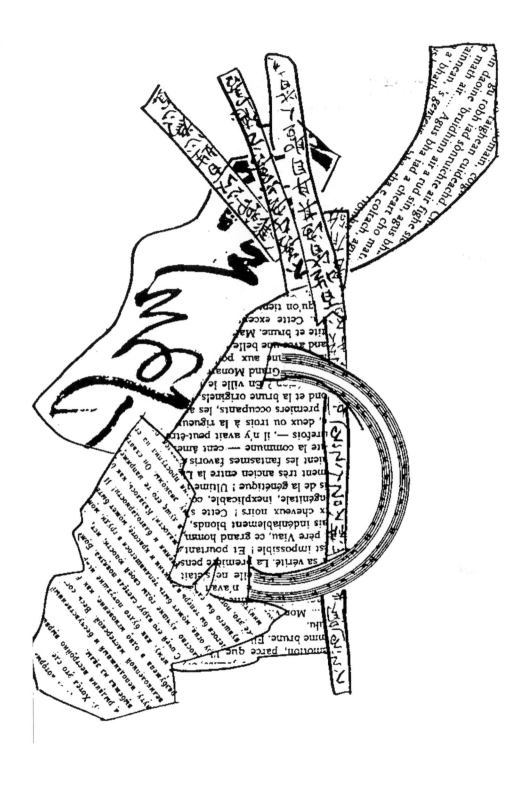

173

              past.a.slaughterhouse...(couldn't.walk)

          w/out....feeling/<u>causing</u>

              pain

        much.bigger.'n.grander
    w/out.clothes.w/out.skin...they.see.too.tossing.hems.
    'n.hind.pictures/the.uniformity.of.each.nail's.crescent.
              the.<u>dirt</u>.of.that.white.splay.&.
                  animal.stirring/
              each.perfect.line.

                  a.stripe.
                      the.nailed.body/
                        nailing.does.not.
                          <u>allay</u>

    handfuls.fell....the.flesh.to.find.water/drawn.
    from.mouth/
              the.mind.is.quite.unsayable

              "<u>entire</u>"

          Extreme.Unction.
              it.came.through.
    plucked.passage.of.headless.drum.
              (weeks.later)...splashed..w/blood...

    the.bay.was.full..FULL..w/inflated.stomach,
        viscera...head.&.feet..<u>SEASPRAY</u>

          an.extra.twist:
              potted........the.jaws.fell.grape/

          peacock...crockery..systems.people.call
                      sickness
                      frogblade:
              accidents....be.it.carcass.of.fulmar...
    gannet.or.sheep
              toppled.by

```
            (mandrake,opium,BLUE.primer)

   "cased".....&.strung.around.the.body

                 pelt
                 (like.kill/the.shortness.of.it)



         the.first.time.

a.devotee....
     (the.safest.way.to.kiss...to.reach)

                 scattering.ragas....
                 bow-wow's....hoola.hoops...
                 thistledown...lost.talk/
                 splices.&.
                           replicas

        of.wolfram.fractures.filleting.the.
                              dress's.navel:

            stomach..spawn.support....the.head.of.dried.ling
            ............child.fragment:



1, 2, 3, 4, 13, 14, 15, 16.

           Every-Day.

           "i.never.told.the.truth.so.i.cannot.tell.a.lie"

                 )
                      (his.entry).a.palette...

        sweet.common.parsley/oleaginous
                      Up.to.Now     (THESE)

     Windows.Open.Simultaneously

                 first.part:................against.wind.....
                 third.move:................the.rain........
                       (his.portrait/her.own.dialect)
```

```
        (blow.of.the.fists)
            on.the.skeleton....

        YAWN/COUGH/LAUGH/CLAP/BANG  (This,the.platinum,
reconstructed version)
            of:
                    (The.Girl)
                    (The.Young.Man)
                    (The.Woman)
                    (The.Man)
                    (The.Men.with.hack.&.burn.methods)
                                                    /
        the.dubbed.voice.of.peasants/
                                    this.one's.a.

        a.a.a.a.a.a.a.a.a.a.a.a.a.a
                            carpenter,


    biting.his/rusting.his.cannisters.for.
                    charge.of.chapter
                                    /
                        change.of.word,

        changed/her.bow/peach.gashed.
        jagged.pounds/the.passing.by/her.house/her
                text.
                was.
                    Exodus




                        the.willow.cages.

    "women.&.all.their.dripping.lace"
    bleeding.insects.at.a.glance/their.name/
    old.roses.among.rock,
        the.full.of.true.civet/

                Cockerel.
                Ostrich.

                    (there.is.no.word.for.
                        SUN)

                            it.is.
```

176

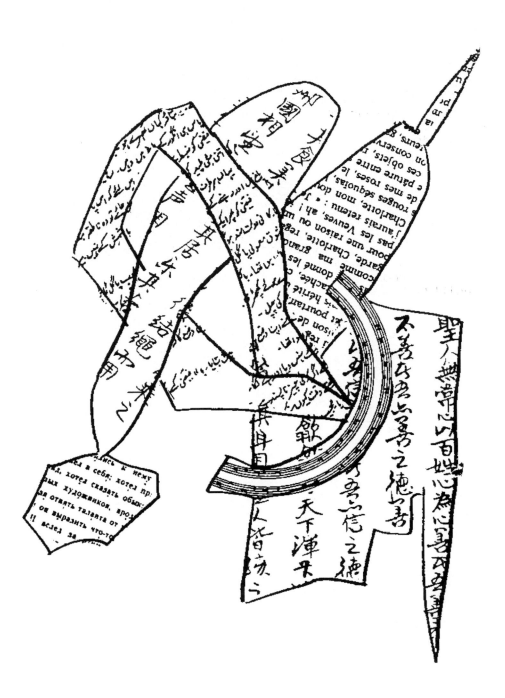

(gone.to.deep.cloud)

He.as.Executioner: (maybe.storm)
                Cut.Thunder.
                Cut.End.
                Cut.with.a.large.Letter.Golden.Piety.

                   (yes.or.no.this.driving.way.of.
                                snakes.and

skull.remain

(long,long.walks.on.the.deck)...
                "to.consider.wearing.

                WHITE"

blue.goosequill.sharpened.fat/fate.of.heroines

"&.then.maybe.you.go.to.another.place"

of.sea........or.river.......of.animal...&.plant

    w/out.minding.blood/gorged.bled.thumps/for.two..
    (knowledge.of.this)....deafening/deading.....

              symmetry
                Redshank/dolomite.
                In.Nomini.Patre.
       the.crease.in.the.fold.of.her.skin's
                            appeasement.
      Unicorn.garnet.ash.

                  Lock.it.Still:

```
Topaz.
it.fills
the.stump/the
                    Sinking.Bones

 "thy.blood.in.circulation"

      its.drapability
              "under
                    her.dress.over.her.heart"

a.bag/
       (an.embalmer's)

          the.small.entrances.by.note/Razor
   to.see.how/she.the.crush.of.each.cage/mending.
      the.blown/bloody.lace.of.them.....


....to.soaring.strangers.....
     (ancient:      medieval:       modern:)
     (mental:       mythical:       magical:)
....the.shorehouse......a.few.stone.rosettes...(briefly).


      the.blade/the.hours.
                    the.carcass/

      the.voice/or.smell.of.hair/the.clouds.closing.in/
      seeing.apparitions/auctions.in.the.open/

          alongside,

      Loadstone
                    /knuckle
                       of.human/hand.in.the.tightness.of.
                          curl
```

Or.............(Memory.of).......

1.   Scorpion

2.   Fox

3.   Ibex

(a.bee.........a.spider.....the.corpse.of.occasion)

        sterlet/diagonal/stain.of.severance/
                        half-open
                         prison

    combs/reticulated/
                    flight/
                        &.other.

                motions.of.bird/
                            shaved/drawn/
                    in.lurch/

                        (to.black)
                        (to.white)

                w/cataract

soda.scones...(HEAVY.TYPE).....rowlocks...ear-lobe/
the.CODAS.buckle.sapphire.Surprise....Mood.of.peakside
alto...lobster.....handfuls.erupt

            (
                ORANGE.rum/the.fanned.red/

)   ....

    of.millet.cinnibar/outlets.FALL

        ("myself.when.i.am.real")

180

```
        in-
  toning.aperture.absence.black.
slit.yr.sad.lanterns
           their.easing.axles
           THAT.cling

"very.near.genital"

      in.meat.scenes.
           "a.ruff.of.white.amusements.on.the.front"

      beCOMING/yellish

              Refusal/&.the.Gardenias.are.as.high.

as.their.roots/
                   to.refuse


      &.be.dispositioned,


           as.flame.....switchblade,
                   covetness.....FUR....
              scattered....fin.chill/
                         CLOUD.BURSTING....

              (Cerulean.Eclipse)


to.kill.........to.sentence....to.pardon...tosave/
the.cloak.of.raw.sorting/someone.dared.to.ask,.the.matter
                   the.face.MASH

   portal/pulsating/grin.swatch.of.hooves/

           My.Lord:

           Type.O:

           Exhibit.P.1:



streetsounds.burn.acquisition/includes.the.violinist/
his.glitter.pour...dying.ladelfuls...cresting.dance.
DANCE.DANCE.DANCE.....
                   DANCE.DANCE.DANCE.....
```

```
         small.perpetual.reds.of.head.&.yellow.scarlets/
         hurling.claw.strut.pigment
                (be.it.fish.mammal.or.bird)


   (he.died.&.then.he.died.&.then.he.

died

   )
```

as.reasons.for.dots.in.the.text:

Rose.Madder.	Roundabouts.
Cadmium Red.	Chisels.
Grey.	Grinders.
Sap Green.	Sirens.
Fuschia.	Fairgrounds.

The.show.of/

Our.Own.Galaxy

its.age.once.more.
Dogtooth/Arrowhead/
Balloon

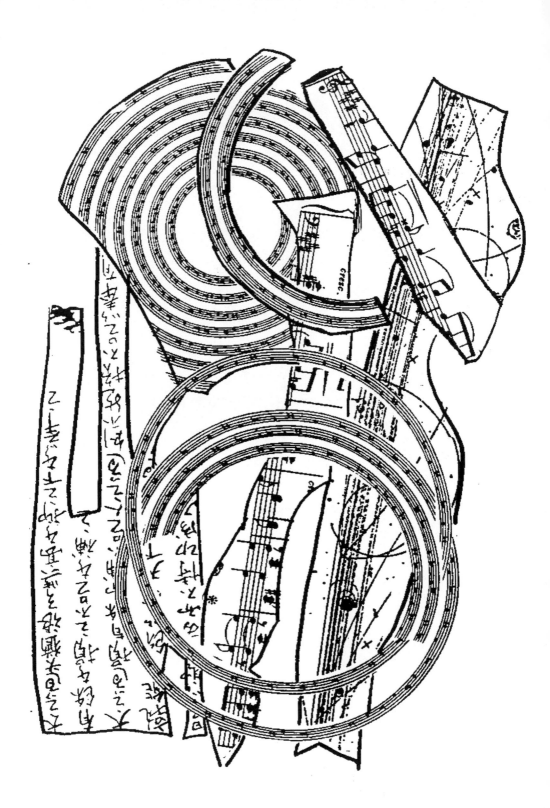

183

(<u>THE.VIRTUAL.CLOUDS</u>)

    correcting.drench.of.walnut/this.act.
      this.disaffection:

(<u>HERE.AN.INTERVAL.OCCURS</u>)

      An.atrocity.of.this.sort.

                  <u>THAT</u>.

undercolouring.voices.as.birth.
   bass....low.....b/neath.....
      green.comes.any.note.you.want....

   for.you?
   for.me?
   for.<u>whom</u>?

these.lamentations.....'O'....Orris...(&.other.
white.or.yellow.applicants)..in.line.between.black.
&.partly.SABLE
     source.of.digitalis..wing.twisted.vellum.
        RATTLE/
            bait-
               ed/snag.the.darnel/
      painted.ace/the.breast,
          its.light....
      arachnid/magnet,lash

 its.influx.of.heart/hard.separations.its..

    <u>Colossal</u>.whipish.nova
      fins.glue.flute.(&
      tuba.snaps.to.free.them)

        CORN-
           cockle.edge.offa
1/
  YELLOW twine: cow.lilt.

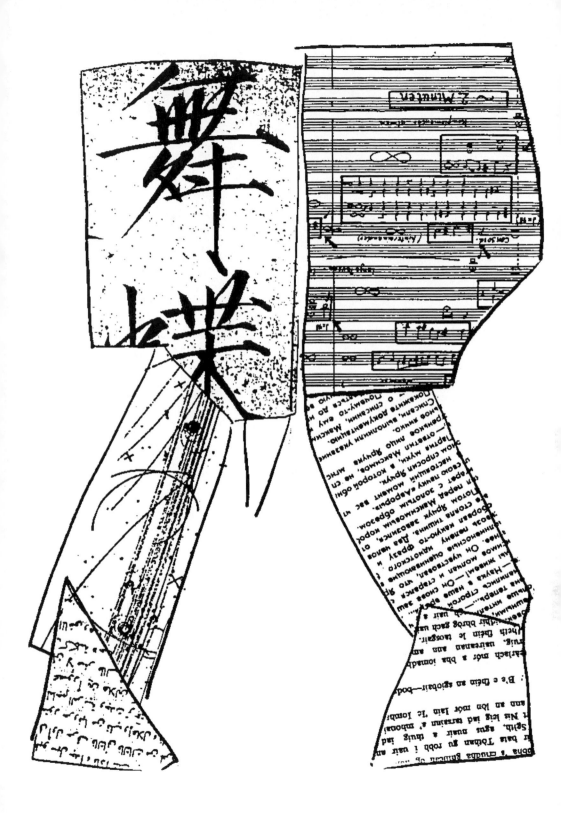

185

'lidding'/rayskin

The.Bed.
spreads.parsnip/the.very.green
pillow.(as.if)....lying.there..
its.fall
its.froth

                    (U,

   "how.does
        your.garden

                    grow?")

DIVISIONS

OF

LABOUR

maggie o'sullivan

For <u>Antony Cook</u>

"Also your tiniest things of you. One is you & all this & two & yet."
<u>from: The Prophet by Alice Notley</u>

THE DISPUTES.

THE WALKS

THE TRAPS

THE FEASTS

THE DANCES.

SEIZURES

THE DISPUTES

```
Damp Air/
Mortar

                (handcart & skirt trailing)
                                Xing

        out/under
   linjag
        chalked pavements
                sorbet FALL-
                        OUT / spray-purse/gothik strop/
                                ribbed musk
                             innard hung pocket


                                OTONO.



            glintzy
                snorting
    silver whorlage/melon amidst
                fine gravel
            sunmix
        tinged w/grey
          mauve elegant, twimnned w/tuppence


    was it

antlers, eye-shell of egg
                twisting where blood is
                        crane jib

                        DOUBLED
                        bonfire
```

Bases bat hunt.REDS burr
throat grave privet/Deep Blue SEE/
        releasing skinblend/Arms

            (did not)

    ribbon leap w/fit trickling neck
            BUT left
          scorpion
             among rock

   kneeling
keening

        Laser
        leica
        leida
        L-E-N-G-T-H/

of anemone / wheat SLIT
                little doorway
            gathering gold it red/making dye/ROUGE Ruby.
            porch wing/
                    scribal piece fluttering/

                    SEPARATION.

            ————————————

        Aphrodite's
         wriggling Flounder:
      inflammable workbook/keepsake/bric-a-burst
            bergundy/beverage sequins leg/notion
                    single gram
        tail/claw/marks/knee
                        PIP
     along sand/
            below

```
        lining to water
             w/out assistance
          making move
                to shared web
           culvert cumulative gown

                    akin
          to tree / Running
                    magenta
                       Longing
              vagrancy To
                       Be
                       Come
                       Un-
                       BROKEN Under


       Nightsilver
       SKYMOON.


              _____


  bisected smoke-whiff
        backstroke/Beatscream/eye thru brain
                    spills
                 Rose Blood
         Gimbal, sunsets twilight & evening
               stars angled thru carob
         Crab Nebula
               Chinese Lanterns, un-


     stealth,
        steel specked aubergine breaks jar/
                    prompts wide wick of ink/
                    fades LIVERSTRIDE lemon
                          divergent
                       cornsheen, harness.
```

ANIMAL DRIP BLUE BLACK BROWN BROKEN
COARSE CHALK CLAY DARK FINE GRAVEL GREEN
GREY HARD LARGE LIGHT MUD OYSTERS OOZE
PEBBLES ROCK RED SAND SOFT SHELL SHINGLE
SMALL STONE STIFF WHITE WEED YELLOW.

Daz.kiln.trigger.boog/erectus,militar/toy's
rim/(by.default)

weeping is
woman as
haven
(all broken line)

Burlap.roadside.hook.(for).amusement.w/rictal
guard.(twinge).food.from
TWIG
this labial pepper

                      stalks

                              Common

          shade,

                  excrement

                          aboulia:

---

coin's other side (will he? won't he? will he?)

```
BLUE RED &
    bordered leaf into north
        drizzled dance/superior clot of
            reedy ringling/
                HUG
                it will....


                        Command

fire/shell/knotted

    Pink after pressing/

                        gamma sheets making night
                            bump upon meat,

                                    Mimosa


        this ear of
            field
            BURNING.


Assimilative.
H(OUR)/the
face whitened by
power & lard, Indigo guts amid flame/flak

        arm/
            gush

                    child/
                        brakes

    peach
        from random  swede
                duet of
                    green/quince
                        anatomies
                            on plain sage,
```

bodies & bodies & bodies & bodies/DEATH'S
                    echo
         carries land

    clear of that dying
                    hostage

struck violet to sham interlude to sham pain

        chested Up
          celadon FIRES

         wound/wounds
    BULLET & CAGE, WAR &

  military purpose/
                bayonet

                    down there
              an old Blood
               impairs ground,
                    roseTILT

                    linearly.

THE WALKS

To record surface, single grain towards
Blatt strips feuilles hojas

    Sepulchral. Jaff, Jonquils
    Ledge. Bearing of head,
    head, cleavage/
    be
      reavement.

        ' Dolls
     Broken into
     Bare bones
     Bore words
          that brought
     white muslin blue peel in just curve red sulkily/
           DARKNESS

penumbra.

      to hear change/cast/choric. (Knot). NOT:

  chance. myth. swish of
stray, feral chance, chances.
      Collusion
        w/movement intending

         drape slippage, tethers

litmus.bonding.
bounding.chagrin.pellets.of.straw/throat.
WATERGLASS.
HARTSHORN.

        Lime
        litharge
        in-

scriptions
of
charge,
        risk/interlocking word under look/skin
         savage light available garden,

                                          peer

     at sludge-lick
             lock

   sundered by

                FACE
        crumbling room dark meat
           pilloried
    (sunlit wind)BLACK,BLACK,BLACK oil.

             ————————————

root of air is

    Owl
  daylight
   dampened Oat broad Core stitch wort/wheat sac
      w/body Open as leaf IVY,
    bruised weave thru sod/compound

                       Pulse

        whipping
    lantern, hyphenated-crystal/clutter-
        BLUE coffin: CLUTCHES. Site of
          DANCE BOWL

     singing Mountain Demon

out/Xes

catchets in teeth

        voice/echo

    where seed IS/held
            broken
    brace of dipthong/
        shot with mauve's

                sweetish disjoin
                        not fern,
                            but
                        cardinal mooring
                            furze-beam
                                from conch/

                                    die wespen.

        ———————————————————————

    Cantilever/lily's damp stare stains glimpse
                inferable
                    bunch

                        of
        rolling
            BLUE   B
                         e
                         11/

            salutes
    warple/gangs lie FRUIT into stillness/Bending.Bruise
            like song ripple
            moody heel of hand
                            was
                    mark of
                        LEMON
                            BLACK MALLOW,

                        WRIST

200

              (& lo, a star)

                   detonates

BLUE ON LID/PINK ON CHEEK
          cheekdripping scree
              carvel/
                   clinker

   saysaysaysay
              saySO
         dill/dash/ -
                   say so LESS.

                   eau de/
              cables.quibble.Bay.crimper.sly
                   tiger.plastics/
                             tiger
                                  plastic

              _____

SEPIA
   easily
 THUNDER
   black saddle of
 hair
       it is
              ...at these encounters...

                        a
                   saddening of the eyes
              & perhaps weep/let RED never tire
                   silled white/white skull
                        pale
                   WING/BEAT

                   of one
              alighting into pool
                        thru
                             dulse

in its meridian

         comb-break,

                                            201

        bough after bough after bough of
anise,
        wrap, _even_ in the smallest words,

        the skin's
             toil
        GREEN/HOUSING winter's

        pounding hull
                old quarters
                        harbour

                breath/_LOVE_.

_____

THE TRAPS

(the reply sublimated)

did i darken yr light?

wound intelligence?

"a wife or daughter knelt upon a hassock, but a gentleman
bowed only his head"

                    it is
                    40 minutes into
                    the film
                    before
                    a woman SPEAKS:
          "everyday i get less
                        than i give"

     a groove/a fault/a pollution/a stigma

Consecration of Tombstone/

                         Other
                         Memorial

        The language was common
     Constructed
             around
                 sexual attraction
          sortilege/mea culpa. mea culpa. mea culpa. mea maxima
                              culpa.

                    O Feathering
                    Fauna
                    snickets

        breath
             quibble
                  commend fig/acorn thrones fire-Arm
                       below replacement
                            level/

204

```
WATERS bring fresh
    lilac to STAND choicest
            gulf in wing
        (other weapons of)

    the stake
round waist arm thigh as if heel & toe
                to be
            destruction


    so,
    sum clouding
under seal of jerking step


            'tis made of

    bundled matchstick
    Oystershell
            "words in the masculine gender
             shall be
             deemed
             to include the
             feminine")


    front-line stuff
            FOREVER
        lustrine/
            war-communiques/pelvises/
        multiple dented
            HYMNEN
            without hurry
                black
            thorns w/ligula brilliant brigs
                nori crowned w/surf
                    deportment




        in turmoil.
```

THE FEASTS

Reading the bottom line. On either side,
natura mortis,
                    gum base: glycerol
                              prints cratered rose

BRIGHT DARK DARK DARK DARK PALE OOZING

                        clotting mechanisms

               RED NATURE of the PULSE

        venous/ ARTERIAL

                BEND

        in wake of

VIOLET/
digs its deep
edge
to
BLUE/its double form held
                          fin
                              swerving
                                  denticle
                              that sort of
                          sentiency
                            fulls anchorage full
                                STOP
                        in wake of window/fingers
                                lay
                            course, replicate

        w/string hook/states of tide
                              banditry

                            unveiling.

                   ————————

ORANGE

Its gel/anatomy of orchid
    earth-skid/wild routes passage/cross
        page, puncturing
    hill red wood early wood edge of
            throat
        close growing
            that little
          trees
        might glow

                    out
                    (after tears)
                    the eyes line/
            Buckle, Hey lo

            BLOOD/BLOSSOM/
                            geemial
                    heat of
                        SUN.

                    ===========

  To possess theories
        of peony
      (PURPLE is red)

 its ragged quench
            support
        Even in carnival, stab
                leached out

                        constabulary/case
                            Palmetto
                        Orchard of
                                salamander
                            crayoned
                                Calamus
                                Sweet Flag

            this ORANGE BLUE MORNING
                    lace
            of shingle/swing of
    corsage/furrowed mulberry/vulva
            bearing

            iris/storm petrel/TRUE

<u>BLUE</u>
<u>YELLOWS</u>

          /   thievery   /

pageants
     against the <u>LABOURING,</u>
                the <u>BROKEN SLEEP</u>

          <u>to consider</u>
          <u>to consider</u>

               the SOLIDITY of
Xeeding whiteness/Xeeding redness

     at ankle/neck/wrist/APERTURES

                    pasted

     headlonginguiseof
     retinue, cordwain making grief,
     wild rice
     the neck's
     twine scissored out
     sublittoral
     thigh
     enfolded in
          wounded arch to wall veridian w/hand & whet
                    fleetspine.

               _____
               _____

     STRETCHES over WATER/catapult rye
               coppery gold
                    egg
                    FREE
                    wood/wedged
                         movements,

<u>SLEEP</u>: <u>SLEEP OF DISTINCTION</u>
               involves

shooting.And.Blinding.

&.BLOW-UP.

               _____

RED / foxglove, redder fire
   thru wood bristle w/single flex
       annulations

       ballooning

blue lateral silk thru garnet bluish/aslant/
cassis awash / linkage
attenuation
zinnia
zip
saddles thickish / known to
shake clear twists, to
tumble
weed / to
bib
dispersal : : : : : : :

       all other fish are
          Lungless, cold
        hawk silt in skin / gunship
      spurted lethal YELLOW
         fire/orange light i wept/
            melon
         herding inward/
      the lash of wrecked

        pennyworts -

from year to year
   entire sermon
      verging on
RED ogen repartee TRUFFLES arbutus / heddled
      record of.

THE DANCES

JEER & DOT
       miss aisle missile mass

                              acre(s)
                                 outnumbing
                                 ----

       chill /

              wimple

                     dandy /

                            lion

Girdle
   of work
 little chamomile
        starflower/soap showered w/mache bite
                              on
                              stem.

To survive
   hurricane
              petroglifos:

                              desert/de-serting
                         ectoplasm playa
                                      combing

              analgesic/accuracy entails

     the dead
        rule each barley bitlet/stoop
   on the half shell, this
           Pink Broad
                  broken jeopardy
        between rose & chequered scag
           RED earth mixed w/Choc-
                                 o-
                                 late

```
    sting Puffer Squeezebox
         nylon
      scouring sun
       flippant splintery
   quail swoop


           perpendicularly

               sparse braking
                       BREATHING

        bark LAPS

over stone wild bread / perennial
                       relatives


          ridden by IVY
                  endive/CRUSH

          PLOP...REACH.THEM...


     REDSHANK, RAFFIA'S cheap turbulence
              telegraphs hay rind,
                              Hey,
                                  arms
                               w/out pause
              trickle white immense hortative
                              margins.



          ——————————————————————



TURPENTINE raiment
    Saxicola
flight paths
         elected to/own hands/more,more,more
               many-headed
                       in-jury


      arms
           ARMS
                 lay net
                             Link
```

                    ARMS do not collide   .

                                               .

                                               .

                    _____

    Appearance
    affirms
    Arnica

            heterophonic/the 'right' position

                    RAINS
    1's/2's/Kick & Pull
            lilac hacking history/disk opaque iron
                    fruits LAY

he /
        lium

    LARKS

                        purr
                    Breakers
            from jester grin/BLURT of

            ink/white presides over purple/
                    spine site
                        bit
                    below soil
                        Banda
rhymed riveting feat/wrung threshold ,

BREASTS are credible,

                              each

    bites nerve/<u>PLANKTON</u>
           <u>BAY</u> bruising/shook mezzo

    less fell BERGAMOT

                yards jaw/
                   broken signal
                bark <u>VERMILION</u>
                      driven thru

        aquatic eye of <u>PALM</u>-belly

        (mardy chive skid slipped shot
                           doubling)

    wool tube,
     twin-spar, Span
   abled deck side box
               loudly

        <u>LOUDLY.</u>
   _____

   _____

RUTS CREW ANGELIC UPSTARTS CRAZE FUSCHIA FROM BRICK BURNT
POPPY BURST BUTTON BUTCHER'S WASTE
   _____   suspended fucking englishes   _____

        weather glut thistle-harness
           whale-tint/kindred marking
                   note
               discontinuous
                     note of

<u>CORNUS</u>

<u>BRUISING</u> / <u>BLEEDING</u>

    alarmed

       man/ifestations

re/

  <u>PORTING</u>

     Myrtle, oldest

        heliotrope.

SEIZURES

Starting from the top (where the Chinese place
the South)

                    CLAY /

                              powdered pure GREEN

            M /

                    BLAZE /

                                        nd

<u>XPLOSIVE</u>

                              Hop
                              Scull/
                              cap/Valerian

            divisions/women/children/<u>LABOUR</u>ing
                              rose/

                              excursionist
                    the skin's dredge/dread

                    <u>horizontal combat</u>

                                        incertitude/

                    hot cress on marble

                    fair votive ALMOND (how air <u>GROWS</u>
quick)

            <u>SILVER/</u>

                              thatching
                              inwards

                              Rain
                    bows foot/fall
                              larval

<u>matt ering</u>

busted

m-e-l-t-i-n-g

<u>mirrors</u>

scuttled cream cuttle behindOPENairs
                    lake w/out/wait/the

                                        SKY   ,

                                              s

    Wingflap
    planting detail
        dialogue
            <u>bridge</u>:

_____

Beginning
  new reigns. Province of tortoise: amber count,
        line/mouth's
            declination

    "to carry <u>its own</u> world where <u>it is</u>"

  Jaw's glace

ladder <u>BRAIDS MEADOW BRAIDS ASH BLACK BRAIDS BLACK BLACK</u>

            Tamarillo

<u>So begins</u>.

BRUISE print,
   CANDID photographs. kids
        CLIMBING / old ships /

   "he loves me, he loves me, he loves me, he ... "

---

water
leads kidney north north moons turtle lune hand the figure
   HOLDS. It is

   rabbit
   laden wild plunge lattice/induced
        goal of two being female & three
            being a male number/five-pointed
                 star

   arming periwinkle:

                 correctness

                 to describe

yesterday/today/tomorrow/
                 as NOW,
            so thoroughly the eye inclining as if to
                 hear
                 by name,

            tree on SKY/belly/

                 stems ironwork
                 of love's
                 trust
                 that i will remember
                 tomorrow
                 is
                 within

      stir of

                    light over wing
                    O raven yr position/going down

                         its demolition

          ghosts which pillage wind/creak
                    fruit strange

            "honey, pardon my sundance -
                         where
              have you been so long?"

                    _____

         LETTERING bloodly seam
              LETTERING
                    of lentil/BLACK
              Lavender dill Lizard claw,

         FWD. VOICING. Voicing Lizard that Lizard.

              Earth of /

                    the STARE /

                              of that Lizard

                                   cribbed chameleon

                    BLUe wooden heels / drum racings

         quiver/quince/bead
              jellied
         astralabe
              Agfa

                    UMLAUT/

                         assembling

         to the right of us, it's the river /

                              RIVER OF.
         _____

         _____
         i swear it: birth was always in the house: i do.

                                                       221

.POINT.POINT.POINT.POINT.POI
.POINT.POINT.POINT.POINT.POINT
POINT.POINT.POINT.POINT.POINT.
POINT.POINT.POINT.POINT.POINT.
T.POINT.POINT.POINT.POINT.POINT
.POINT.POINT.POINT.POINT.POINT
.POINT.POINT.POINT.POINT.POINT
T.POINT.POINT.POINT.POINT.POINT
.POINT.POINT.POINT.POINT.POINT
.POINT.POINT.POINT.POINT.POINT
.POINT.POINT.POINT.POINT.POINT
T.POINT.POINT.POINT.POINT.POIN
.NT.POINT.POINT.POINT.PO
.POINT.POINT.POINT.

.POINT.POINT.POINT.POINT.POIN
.ANK.BLANK.BLANK.BLANK.BLANK.B
BLANK.BLANK.BLANK.BLANK.BLANK.
BLANK.BLANK.BLANK.BLANK.BLANK.
LNAK.BLANK.BLANK.BLANK.BLANK.B
BLANK.BLANK.BLANK.BLANK.BLANK.
LANK.BLANK.BLANK.BLANK.BLANK.B
LANK.BLANK.BLANK.BLANK.BLANK.B
BLANK.BLANK.BLANK.BLANK.BLANK.
BLANK.BLANK.BLANK.BLANK.BLANK.
LANK.BLANK.BLANK.BLANK.BLANK.B
BLANK.BLANK.BLANK.BLANK.BLANK.
LANK.BLANK.BLANK.BLANK.BLANK.
ANK.BLANK.BLANK.BLANK.BLANK

RANGE.RANGE.RANGE.RANGE.RANG
.RANGE.RANGE.RANGE.RANGE.RANG
RANGE.RANGE.RANGE.RANGE.RANGE.
.RANGE.RANGE.RANGE.RANGE.RANGE
RANGE.RANGE.RANGE.RANGE.RANGE.
.RANGE.RANGE.RANGE.RANGE.RANGE
RANGE.RANGE.RANGE.RANGE.RANGE.
.RANGE.RANGE.RANGE.RANGE.RANGE
RANGE.RANGE.RANGE.RANGE.RANGE.
.RANGE.RANGE.RANGE.RANGE.RANGE
E.RANGE.RANGE.RANGE.RANGE.RANG
.RANGE.RANGE.RANGE.RANGE.RANGE
.RANGE.RANGE.RANGE.RANGE.RANGE
ANGE.RANGE.RANGE.RANGE.RANG

O'SULLIVAN 1984.MAGGIE O'S
MAGGIE O'SULLIVAN 1984.MAGGIE
1984.MAGGIE O'SULLIVAN 1984.MA
LLIVAN 1984.MAGGIE O'SULLIVAN 1
IE O'SULLIVAN 1984.MAGGIE O'SUL
MAGGIE O'SULLIVAN 1984.MAGGIE
AN 1984.MAGGIE O'SULLIVAN 1984.
SULLIVAN 1984.MAGGIE O'SULLIVAN
IE O'SULLIVAN 1984.MAGGIE O'SUL
84.MAGGIE O'SULLIVAN 1984.MAGGI
LLIVAN 1984.MAGGIE O'SULLIVAN 19
GGIE O'SULLIVAN 1984.MAGGIE O'S
N 1984.MAGGIE O'SULLIVAN 1984.
O'SULLIVAN 1984.MAGGIE O'SUL

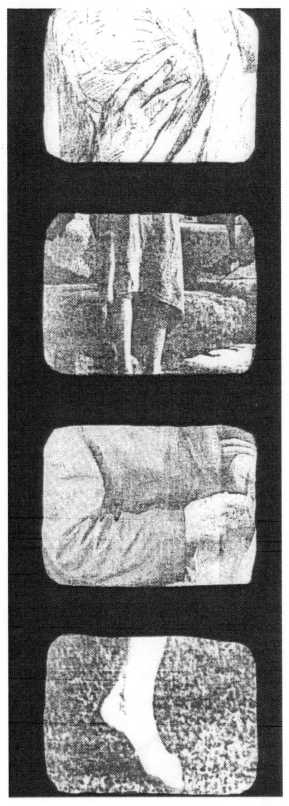

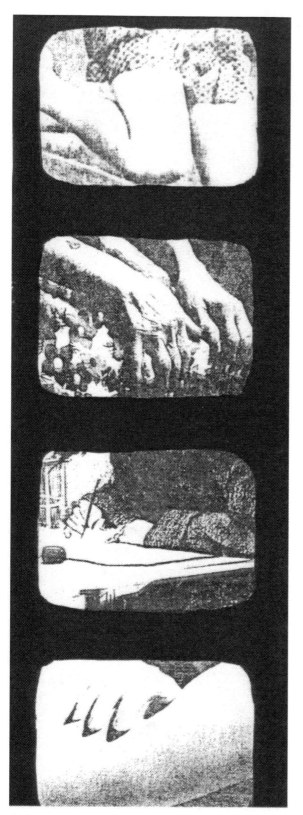

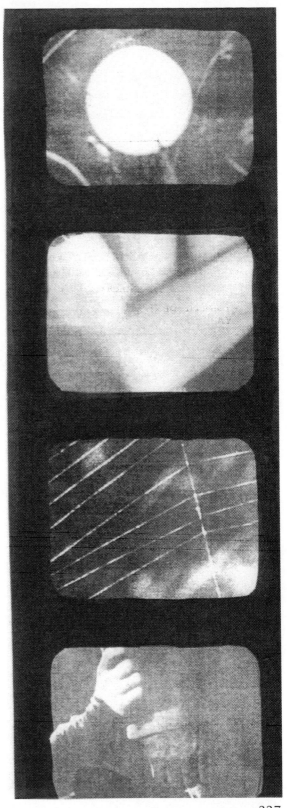

227

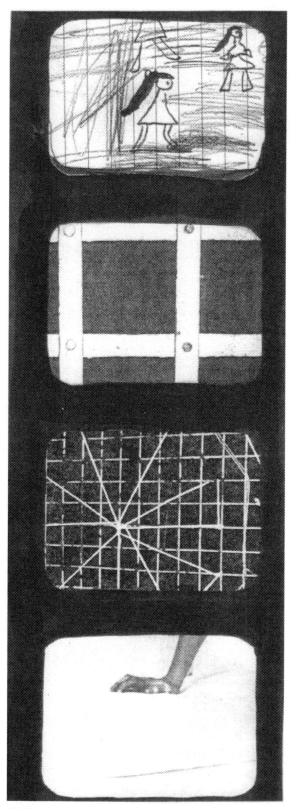

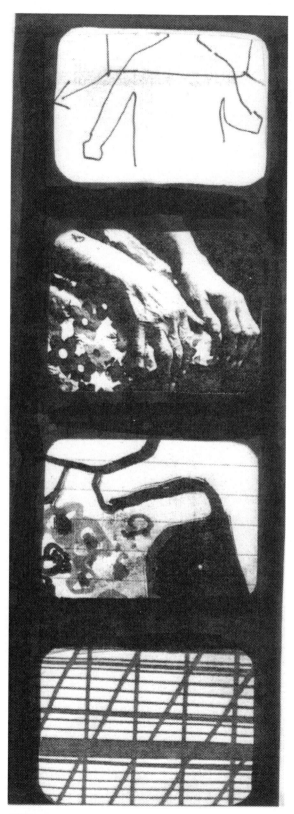

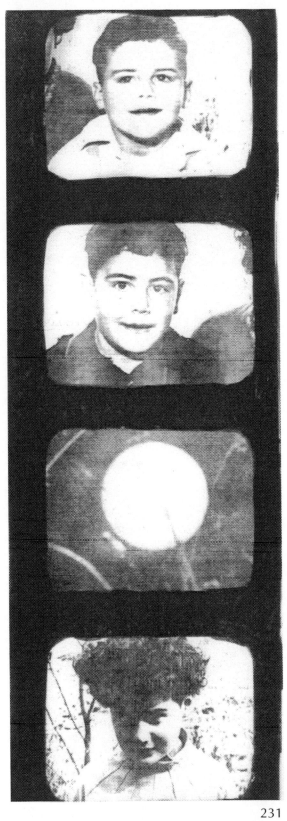

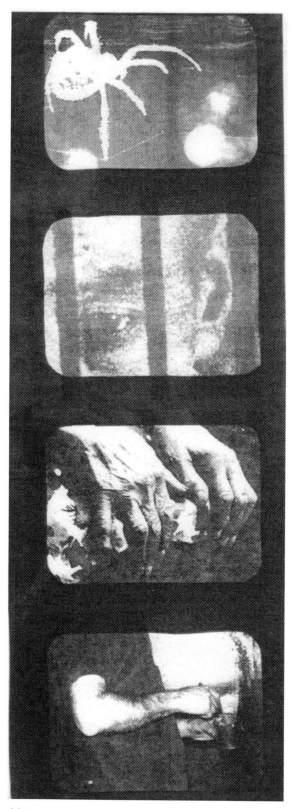

234

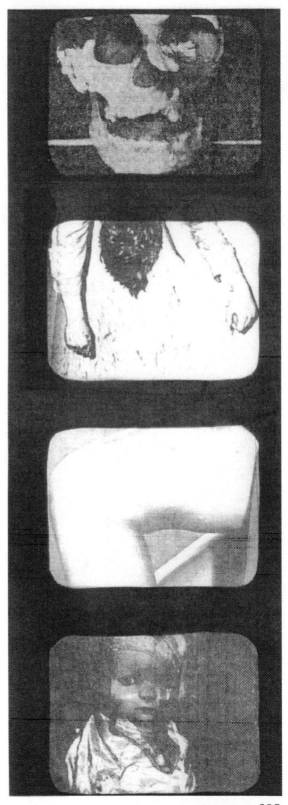

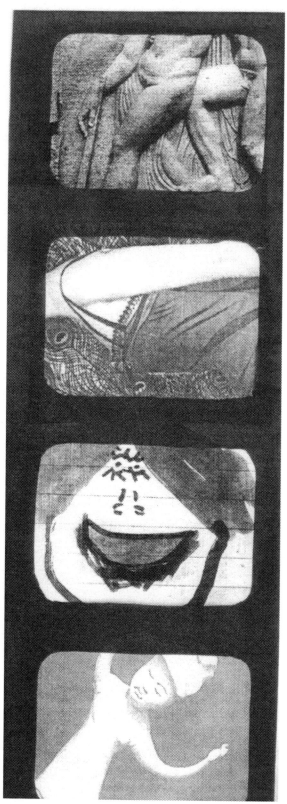

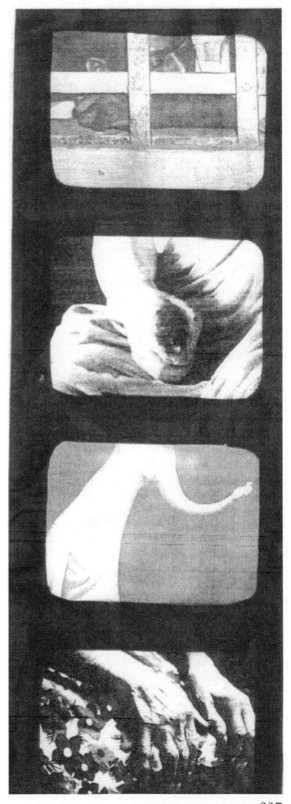

237

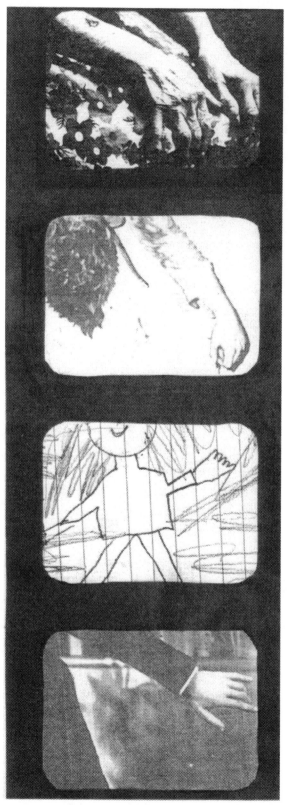

240

242

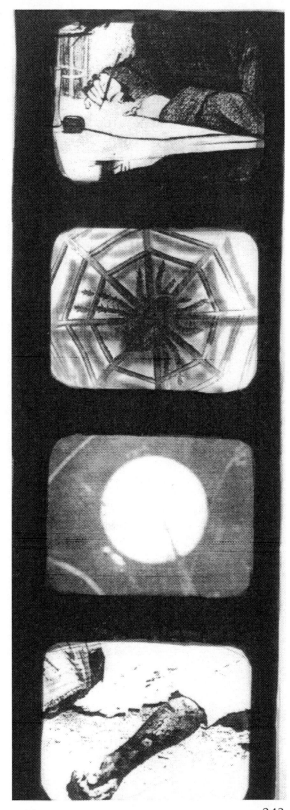

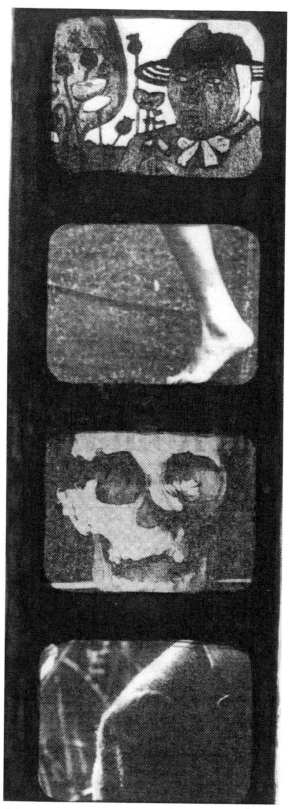

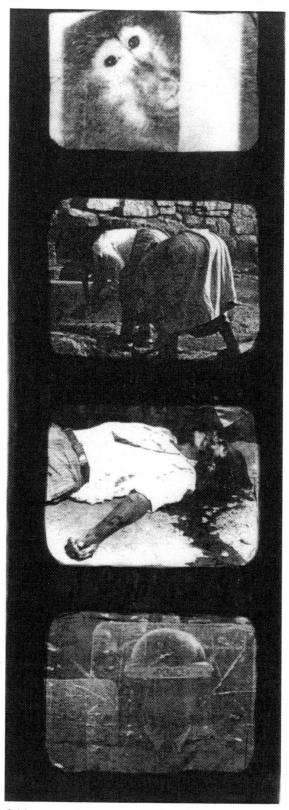

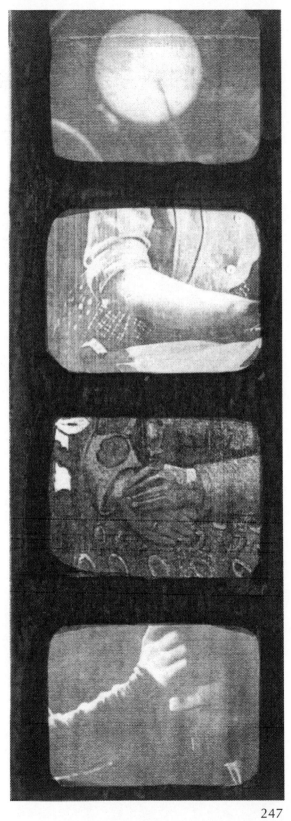

248

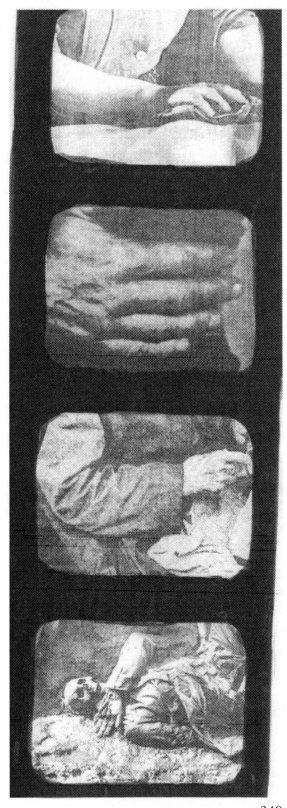

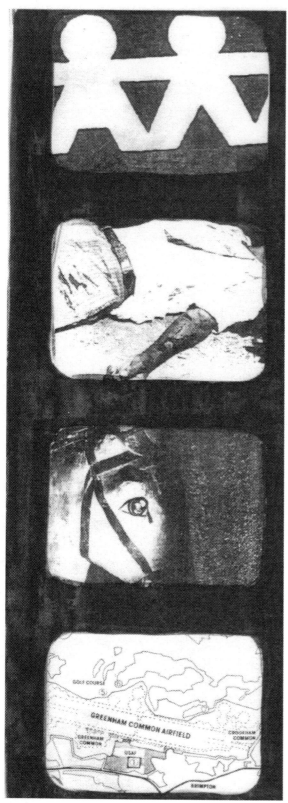

250

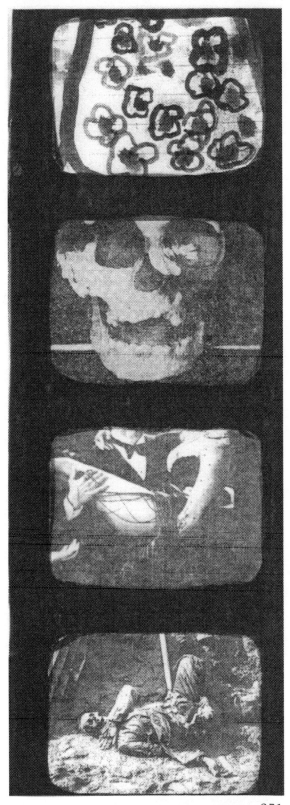

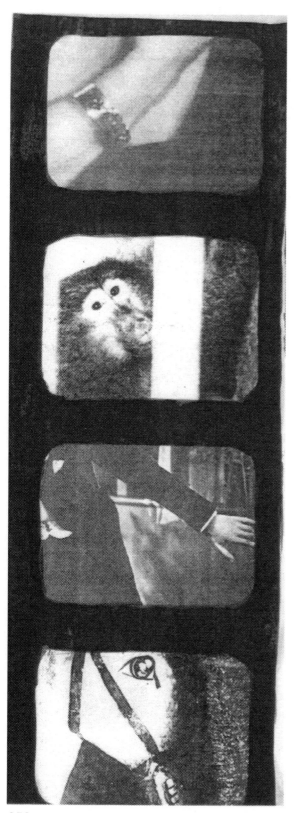

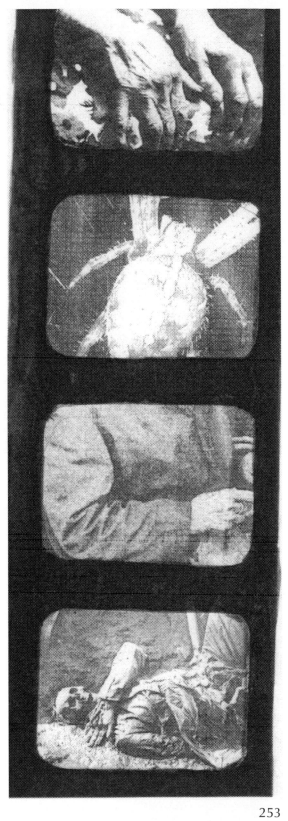

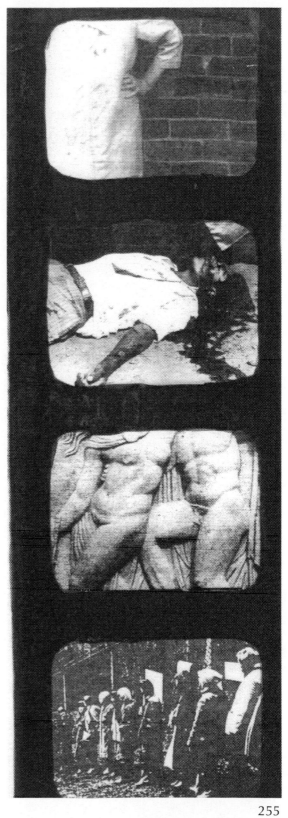

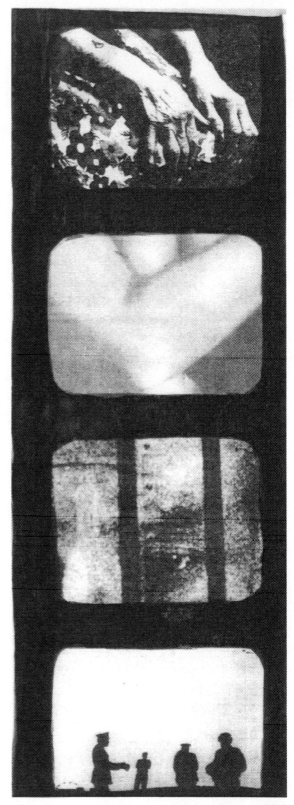

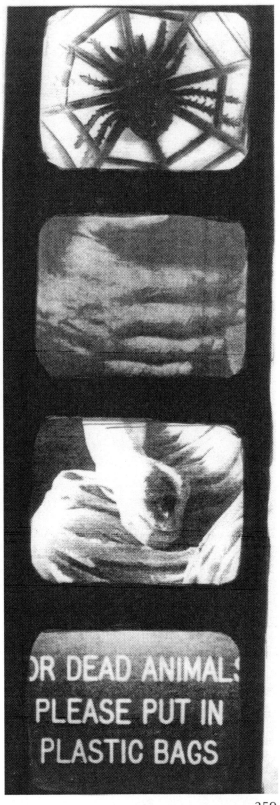

259

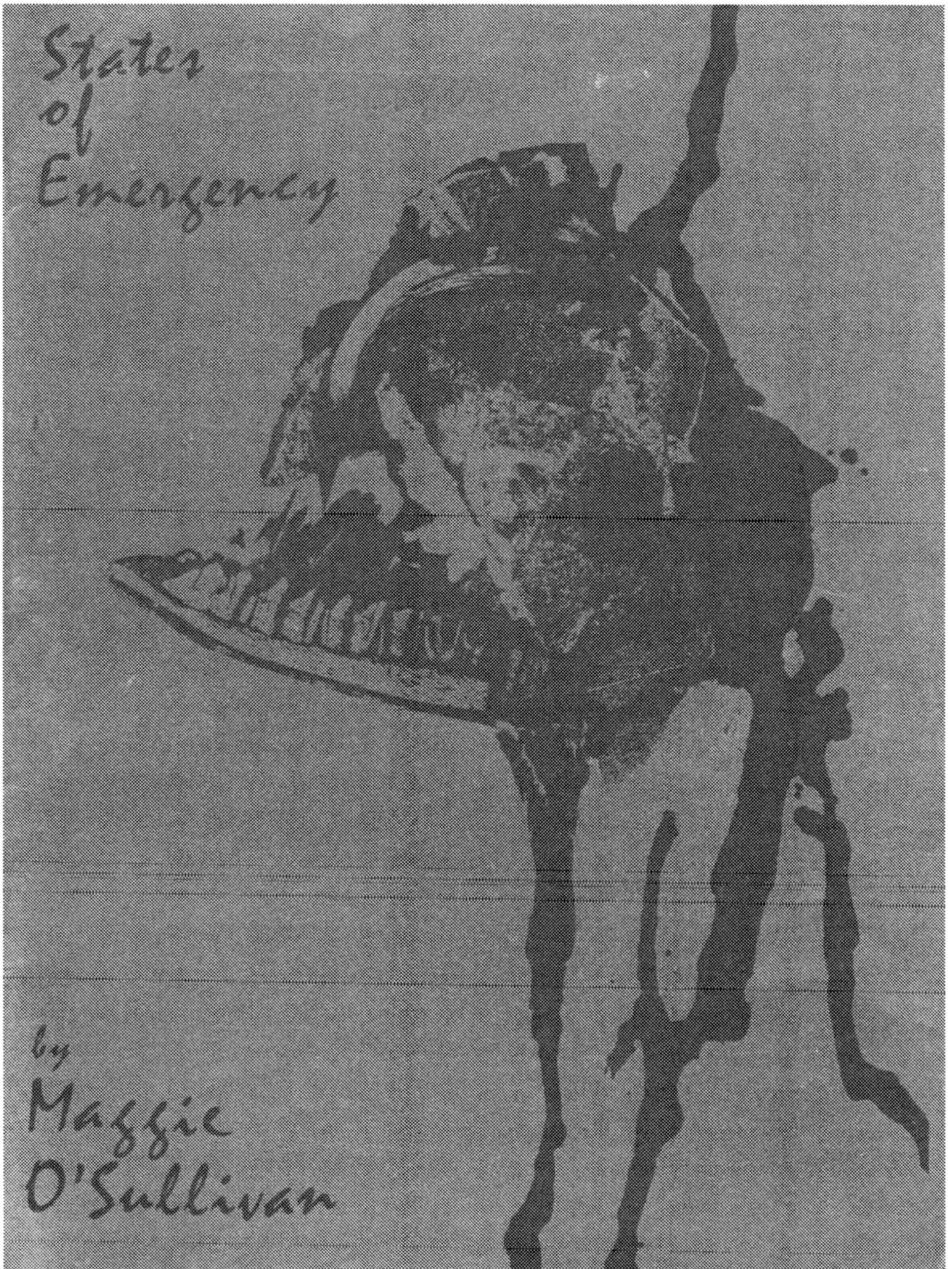

States
of
Emergency

by
Maggie
O'Sullivan

For Barry MacSweeney

"an eye for an eye - in the end the whole
 of the world goes blind"

.

(Graffiti: canalside wall,
 Harrow Road,
 London W.10.

Good Friday, 1985).

1. Lottery & Requiem

2. Headlights

3. Busk, Pierce

4. Plight

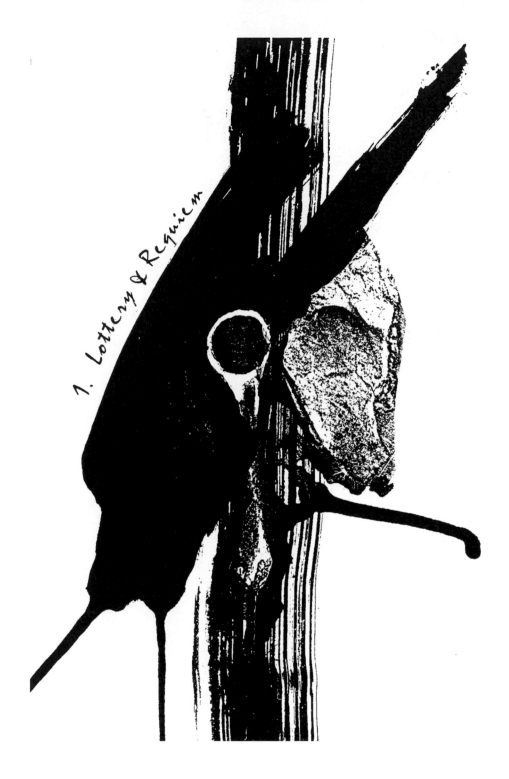

1. Lottery & Requiem

(<u>for Basil Bunting</u> : 1900 - 1985)

    pot lilac,
      pet thorn
      <u>flick</u>
        nest

back,

<u>BLUE BLACK BLUE BLACK BLUE BLACK BLUE</u>
                      <u>BLACKED</u>
      Night bloods
    putted rowdy roundeth liver

        laund

      The Amber
    bidden belly amidst
        cry
      dustling,

            peril/pebble
           <u>endless</u>
      reed, the day w/persimmon

                Flex
raw, woollen hungering.

      Broke Paper.
      <u>Larch Warblage</u>.
      ladder & ladder
    Conifer, come caistor, crowle, winter
      in creases

      the bound paw.

2. Headlights

                    lingual radius,
                         the mouth's reSTAINED
                              Briar
                         Suckled Monstrous
                    Plunge of Wing.

                         Hollage,
                    BLOODLYING
              leper bitted ribbons twist   ————
     Hideous, horrored
                         held-in
                    hurts
                         fuck & tear/
                         hawk & hammer/
                              rupture, keep ————

savage contraventions   ——————————

Pull stomach
rhumba crimson
rhumba
Does for

what is distant   ——————————

                    LONGEN
                         O
               Soured Crucifisted
                    HELLS.

falcon/

        quicken/

              trippant/

<u>CLAPPED PALADIN PURPLE ENACTORS</u>.

        teared mantles
      tug holly Twistfuls
              Tart,

        <u>ICENED CHIMES</u> ——

<u>be</u>/GUN/<u>be</u>SCREACHING

          caged mollusc - cracked out in
              thistled bangling liver toxic
                cannibal quicklies ——
                  pluck vision

    jeer Tar Cloth
        chain jay-
           flared
           <u>PUNCH BLOOD</u>
      nailing Choke
   enforced ignitions ——
          quell of the starving.

```
Bier ——————
The Spilt Reels ——————
            Bannying Ashery,
        Diadems Astir -

                        SKINT
                Styx/
                    Séance Burly
                        Sunned Arrow
                        SKY
                mink
                    seeped w/
                            ROAR ——————


                                O
                    mad, sad
                        mansion


                                O ——————


    Malingering Star ——————
        bearing skelped gripped
                elders, lighted
                    Raddle Bullion
                        FISH/
                    dead
                            Glasters
                teethy bleds -
    bleeding, ever bleed - BONES -
Pan tatters rotten alert caresses,
                        colada songs.
```

Glissade & Spire.
Candelabra.

Confessioned

Belongings.

Incisions

goulding
coiled grave, mixed
Sheave
heel scorch ———
How Proudly
Sorcering Beat ———
Torture Leaves Mark.

BLOODEN PLUMMET

Sheave
Blooden root
Double Bloods Go Black
Gealed Clapper,
Cloughsmut

Banked w/Precipice ———
w/toiled
Stark Jugger Noughts ———

blasted bewitchments —

tomb surgery.

```
          Whip Teasel Bleeded
               Cunningly,
               USE YELLOW
          Noise the Sand.
        Spoked Rivenstuff.
     How Bladden Duffled
               Burning
                    is.
                    is
          buyed wove ribaxe/
                              other bones
                         lining to midnight,


                              still,


          stunning lulls
               shiver
        Thorned Hoyle ─────────
     Vicious Familiar Letters ─────────
          LONG LONG LONG LONG_____
               Long
                    O
          BLACK HINDING
               blue
          canny noise
                    O
          Dammer Curves
               panting
     Mad on puffin peltpath
                         peltpaths to
                              defecation.



MOON LACINGS
```

GO
LOCK & RAG INTO
LETTING

Freen Lot. plie,
minus numbers

"the oppression, the insanities"

fringed Rhumba tongued War

mix on
bergundy bestial Jury all
white margins
locked out Acro soloing

whip, galley
stacking
Authentics.
Unauthorised
Bleeding.

Give & they flesh.
scrubben eels in the soul undressing
sinister fists, barbed
double shadow, bouldered kill w/moving

Octave:

                        Sequencer,

Crow, classified carrion, wafered plunder

beacon loned w/sea severely:

gullen butts

<u>BLADE COMBUSTIBLE</u>
claw splendour

assassinate, back

<u>appellations</u>

Jag Venge, Joletta.
cuffed ivy.

<u>Lamentations</u>.

blowdy louring legs from under: LEAPT, SHONE

<u>them sort</u>:

Bucketed Butcher
spitting stiletto Smiffy Piss of Dahlia:
plucked, fucked,
BLACK THE TEST
Broke Out,
<u>under needle</u>.

        grisled gales
          (shh,
        Poppy
      Latch Rat/Tremor/
        Tremblant
   tilting mace, rampant bake of
           LICE ———
           BURIAL ———

          <u>TOLD TO</u>.

Arrow
Carnals Clench
Broth

cripplage/Cloud SOUNDER

Songing
Stashed Whelk
Hibble Struct
BLACK
Rapping Lily Up Side/
Owl/Crow Quantum Curse:

wounding
Elage,
Tart
Amazing Absence:
pull over Tannoy

enemy lines
rip
rocks will corona

caverned
JET ruther,
arcy bend before
culty sautéd coasting,
AXE
flew tinned rock tarred conch,
clude storm,
cullen stayed

no proper employment.

CRAWL ROOK.

Bleared Flint, inch by inch,
been gather bone, piggery.
Brokens.
mint & judo.

                Flexed Necker, Bell Haslet,
                            widened laudanum
                                    stern furze
                                    frillSING
                            be/WILDER/beast
                                    RED
                            by lilysong:
                    haunt Flutter pale,
                                    gardant.

                Raw drowned coupling
                        moths
                    phlegm
                        treed, unpleasy ━━━━
                            to stomach,

                    broken boll-
                                o-
                                naise,

            drove
            BLEEDING

                to   ━━━━━

Many Salt Silted Hitting Twisted Glass Reprisals.

                    Talked
            cuts ditch to the head,
                    brang passages,
                         breath halves
                         HANGED
                    heart cross lung

Magma fire. Burla lithic. Black pansy. Orna dotting.

                         Haunt
                    sonorities, algid
                         placing

                                   soured White

                              havoc

            Shug Moon,

                              donkey's years

      drawn éclair, fucked branches.

3. Bush. Pierce

Injure Tinglit

fusen deam stroboscope deam skidder

           TLOKETS
        mourn, leaden

         belenders
        lie & blister ———
    fetched silvers, these
            NECRO
        gutteral gardenias ——————————

          screed
        sneak tintering

        Grief Entry.

        Lick O,
      badgered Rioja, carving

           vulned butchery,
                face
          impaling wing
        each buckle
            quilted flute
                  lemoning
                    catched
                  ICY florist,
    X/tinct-
          ure

      w/Sea,

          dead violet.

Jagged Pebble Song.
Unlawful
Cliffs
Will, where no Cliffs be.

woundlark.
moochpennybreeze.

                         O
                   how the filthy
                     Keepsakes
              Truckle Back Tripling
                       Ash.
                Ink, launjer, red on leash,
                     BLOOD.
              Crooked Swatch(ish.yellow)———
                   Fling Flaunden
                     Sheenies
              Quick Poppy Tie of Axe ————
                   Drumcut strip strung twists
                         brooch
                           &
                pen Funerary tabletter, armistice,
                       Drown!

Keep
Geographies.

1	2		4			7	
	2	3	4		6		8
1			4	5		7	8
1	2			5		7	
		3	4		6		8

canker tap, olive ashake, Tranced
AXLE,
candy, the bridle ————————
fever, the train ———————————

helted INDIGO

HAWK
Bloods Bleam

STRIKED
Purple,

tree
BLURTING

choux crab, ryed hare,
Soot Squeeze ————————
Clouted Triksty Gutter ran —————————
to Stone.
Crimson. Cockerel Cream. Tinker Tub.
Dolly Puke, Doily flak, Pinnie Gullet ——
KISS MY ARSE ——

rebellion
backwards.

FROWN RAVENS
Peak Nerve

NUMB w/ripened give ——————

the SKULL'S

own

stark

jurried

storm

cracks Gleed ——————

inadequate coal

—————— Glaud

gutted w/Jet ——————

fraudened harriers Punch

&

Beat

fowled moorage,

one cerise woken skin,

one bone of that

zigzag, plateau, zigzag

GRIEVED, GROUND,

knarls move/Expulsions Deal/Galliards

Brung,

FLAME & WILDERNESS.

(for Joseph Beuys)

Conjure
alumni.
      (Swan Violet
        SPIN
          Clacky Sable:
      Root Swirling Lamblet,
   Stunden Jugend. Severed ribSAD
        Ivy Spike.
      GEISTLICHES.
   arms round
rip/weather grunt/scab chant
          wound/WAKED
      CAUSTIC ERASURES.

      stone joins
     this barren place
   LOOPERLY broth/do trick on me
    thorn under

    Crack Open
     Ox-gauze,
Clash kindling jumped liver,
       bruise-
      raiment.

        O
     Loden
Borage w/the Bees yew straight-bellied
    combatants ————
crieth among purple volant ——————
  wing

   rags
     FLARE ————————————

     Burn/ALL grimey blood ——
beast epic fuses of death.

Sea Gave Up
Ripped Reaming Wills.

Barked Broken
Batten Meats/Hartle Sinter:
Moon Leaved,
Moon flank
flim by Anger. Glenz: got,
Gagged
Rope:
Rotch purpled grease
glooming.
Mulberry shook.Stone plus rain.
restless,
DOWN. DOWN. DOWN. DOWN.

Dragon Diamond Rollers flouting
Celled Coin.
Jewel Vampire. Double Windy:
SKY
bits ──────

Rip.

flames
claw
body petit-point / nail's
coarse
jeered jute ───
hilted fuse box, any bunch ────

dyed muslins ─────

comed iris.

DAYE.D. DAILY-NESS.
abdicator, incendiarist, relinquisher,
tatterer, batterer, menacer, heretic,
hooligan.

                    a/BROAD
                bloody lymph

            gullens plum w/fur:
                BLINDINGLY ————
            clart w/mesh
        Clouted Moor/Common Wood

    SkullSICKY

                SICKENslough
                SKAPApeg

                Pound & Roar
                Dart & Grieve

                BLINDINGLY ————
        Crushed Moon Suffixfuls
                of Wire
                    It Be/
            stark penury rock:
        GREAT Janning BURLESKES
                Brick LITANIES
                            bricktresses
        fap taw, glass & flex —

    shawlswound, brace of inky bat ————

                  hook lily-Rippering
                       savage
                    brooding scab

                        BLEEDINAL

          BANNED BANNED BANNED BANNED _____ __
                              helpLESSly BLACKING

                        Last Return
                        Kept Possession
                        Left Crevice ————

                        CRUSHED WOOLS

              wattled slare————
                      pull sallow sickening
                            Poppy ———
                        Shackle Flaring
                         keens crank
                          iron-held
                             head ————
                        Baba Paving,
                              Hang Foundry,
                         Dance
                 into stone: Elm Sackler:
          Sea Lage, Red Stroke, the Kots
                              Harshlicken
                                  muscle, Grind-

ERY/

Crooked Asp,

LAND PIECES, LAND

UN-EDGE

Planteen, Paper Splashed Cutner

HAWK

It Broke. Oyster. Eglantine.

Tuttle Weave)   unweave

codling   )   colliding

ASH

Wolvers Maunch

the light

w/Nick & Shadow, rag Vile Stunt

whiten s Hack

& suicide

GOBBLE. GOBBLE. GOBBLE GOBBLE

starling fuzz, fucking derailment.

Bloody dead

decased hells

less human

SNARE crimed, hems conch-ETH bleed

flock, dis-ease

Tarred & Take/

Beyond

wound

Common Destruction,

utter

cook root : tormenting conscript

Coup de'etat.

Chippenscab,
     another
    Moon's Right Agony ——— ——

  <u>BE HOLD OUR</u>
<u>BLOOD, BE HOLD OUR THROATS CUTTING</u>
                blace lace, Breath Cloudage
                   hammering
              crocus into stone
               raw coil
        Confections - lie cliffed ———————

    clashed/
      bloody cotton
        clotty halo ——————— ——
      dreg larcenal/Hack holes,
          <u>MUTILATION</u>
          ajar
        this day ———

   BLOOD RAN
  Breathbills, Box Hardfern,
markness, pay thing, every
     draught of oyster
       Struck-Eyed Coal—————— ——

             <u>THE EXPELLED</u>
  w/Teller's Cage ——
  drenched lesion.

Teddled Skirtish Gut, menaced silver/
        Sanged Aspen/
        lock arms
    flogged, snake-a-stole, syllabub —————————
                            tram There.

    JET —————————
        Tiden Twilt,
            Pitch Jutted Wire

                plumbed
            solutions walk —————————
        Bitterspat needles pull
Projectionist's Beam - thorn storm, turn killer,
        Kicked Curt, Stinted
        Drag Ocean; OTHER.

        ————————————————————————

Descant. Painsong. Stoop of Dagger, Gargoyle,
        Fluddspun Gryphon—————————

                Juniper
                winters
                un-
                    fold —————————

    crunched calico stanchion,
    Swirlvinegar, SWIRL, SWIRL, SWIRL, SWIRL
            gunned WITHY giant —————————
            Barnacled nausea,

    ————————————— Flodden.

Drake Styed. Chorus,
     Shelterer's Cardamon.
   Calliope, Calyx, Chowder. Trashy fet & BOLT
            Daily ————————
         Threadwork & Ribbon
       Plait on Rock
        SPIKE
      Six and Six.

Gonna <u>Be</u>.
<u>Just</u> Gave.
     <u>Sherbet Deals Crow, Deals Crow</u>,
      <u>Slag Deals Deathy Rabbit</u>.
       Shark Furl.
       Suck Vile Brick.
     Knife in the Jaw,
        Lies in the Questioning,
            Cloaken Snow
             <u>STILL</u>

    Circusses.

————————————————————————

The Suffocates.
The Strangles.
The Terrifies.

   <u>WATER Heightened w/BODY</u>
   <u>HEART Heightened w/CLUTCHED OAK</u> ————————————

```
        Errant Orations
                throttleback, VERY, VERY
        beggard bang
                as blood
                upon ships ───

    Paprika Mist w/fig stone grin ────
                ROT PERFUME
                LIVE SEX ──────────

                EXILE


        & the starred
    cough is TWIST & GRAVEL


────────────  GOLDENER SEIZE OF ASH/SOURSLATTED GUNFENCED
CARDINAL WATER/EYE OF MAMMAL ───────────


────────────SLAMMED Kill/Rib
                Shack Ruby/Broke
                    over WING


────────── BUZZARD


        is the ear ────────────


            in pulse
        pleating attendance

    across caged
            vermilion

    Skull's Black dlinted


                STEEPLE/HOUSE OF SLEEP/COBALT ZIP
                KNIVES
                        cut,
```

```
zinnia jag w/meat ————————————
      uncased
  hipless waves
        vomit:
      hurl colours:
        hook & mix ——————————————
```

STRIKE lazure

```
      limb from body/Vessel/
                Valley Curtains Gaunt


                  & HEAR ——————————————————

  tinter-stand,
      ruptured Blue stoned slurry ————————


              Pig Flood.


      Shante Flexors. Snatched meridian,
            vault/
                snared
                    hail ——————————


  Cantabile, Inverted quartz,
Grilled Rage of nail/tide of ————————————
              grim torn internments ————————————————
```

BLITZSCHLAG:

```
So numerous,
        the Banded Stuttery Traffic ————————
              Lung  Fanched
          Fugitive Speak of Dying.
```

———————————————————————————————

.

unofficial word

maggie o'sullivan

"We stand upon the brink of a precipice. We peer into the abyss – we grow sick and dizzy. Our first impulse is to shrink from the danger. Unaccountably we remain". Edgar Allan Poe

"Language is not simply a vehicle for representing one's time, but a material force in its creation". William Carlos Williams

Under the Yellow Iris –

    land

        seizures –
          oval shields/
            HAMMER
          fists **Xplode** –

May Down.
Hollow Fern –
LIVER,

      this ease,
        this thug-limped cloud
          COLDEN
        COMEY VIAL:

BEAT,
   BELLOW
      me Cloth/
         Shakings of Chisel/
            Chounded all pitches –

      trembled
       in-
         laid
      Broken O's:
        GREAT
      halten gangings
         Utter-Ably vestment:

      Crou ched &
BLEATING PLACE.

             SNOUT
  spittle,
  & the raw moon
  soothly addled
          scourer to grim
           littlest flood they
       Bubble & STOLE scarab
         Poise on Dunces.
           Policy Speech
             Haste-Bones
               trickle out, the
  Blisters
      churl from a far Ledging:

Silver Dawn of slippery leaves & snow: Some
do not bend
ground, ground
pearling
pearling

pieces.

✣

Riven Mephisto Tabla Smashing.
Spear Gut.
Ball & Spike.
Frieth & Skirmish.
Cruels & Broth.
Pale Shoed
Paven Tower
Bents

Diagonal.
Gamut Arsons –
Bloodiest groping –
GONE SONG,
SWOLE CLOWNERY,
Dagger Breakish
Clenched Low
placements.
"they are no shoddier than hot.
they
peddle. took me on".

Day in day out –

flared

yammer suck w/a system/
aplesick slipping thru sleep/
so skeletal/
so

Brinks
OF
SHADOW

Brinks
OF
jangled palmery, horrible
jabbering
twisted Removers/tin-tin
Scraping
vexes –
leaf
into thistle/

reviling

occurs.

RAIN STUFFS.
SAME,
cry opposites.
Betweens. BETWEENS.

        Scattered
        paper city Reds/Half-Moon Done
            Chemical –
    Great crackles on meridian:
           cuckoo locks to
      elephant:
         HOWL.
        walk on rock,
          face
        the stricken
    fumigate Coders now –
          Blackish Lenten Boundaries,
              Guardia:

              *

Skullset.
Dead Wolf Ear.

Cliff Jostle, Beak

    (& broke of it so)

Tomb gold
twine
sank into
Grave Tellings, Twelvings –
    convulsed

crimsony terminal clusters –
             Cladders & sapling
             Brooding & bringing
             TIN SNOUT.
             TEN THATS.
         Thresh-on-a-Stump.
         OPENS, CLOSES, OPENS, CLOSES.

Rupture.
Scaldey Will. Soarsaway: Drakestuff
& Primus: so that: & thus:
Patient Larded Bitter Carmines,
Mimosa,
Clauses to Memory.
Words to Chant

             (Today
         weeps) bowing, scraping
             Up ladders down
             yell ERRth:
                 "poorest of twiners"
                 the Sky Arsenical

             GLUE BURSTS

         Precious Animal Kinship.
     Dystrophies.

how the eyes are made

Dead Eye Dick's.
Cash When You Die.
Cash If You Don't.

Hath Eaten,
a leg, an eye, orange voyages:
fins
in the flesh
of infinite fracture.

Words wiped out,
shattering clasts,
Summonses,
Disturbed Dimnesses, gorges.
Explicit compleynt.
Gust Raiders, Doned Primaries, Lurch Curatives

Shiver Riddles
Ever Vicious

AILSHELL
hunched Lake boneded
wingy calms
garned upward
Death
clouting girded vein,

ALL CROW POSITION –

countless, cloven ravines –
     NOUGHTS knived –
   Chippering out
    into

claw, claw,
   chortle arcane
     CLAW TONES, blundering
       ablutions,
     dreadful accuracies,
       kiss plurals,
     blueBLIND tinkling,
       frown
        ALERTS –

so governed,
   so –

These alarms & warnings –
These spears & crippletalk & Creeping bitter
fouled knots among Fulled Stars –
These warned Dews Be
    doomed shed –
       jean moss.

     JANGLE T. JANGLE T. JANGLE T.
      bottomless igniting –

These chuddled double-ones coughing slaughter –

Ring. Ring. Gang. Gang. Gones, Done
of all the Unseen Tinies. Hulce Hake jeering
pussives, chauncy globe-a-gapes,
Curses & Clusters.
these multiplications –

      These moanings. These fixes of scum
      smeary lipTHEFTS –
      These glove deadner/overSIGHTS of ear –
      These moanings –

These Tramp Saffrons
      tampered,
      Thorned
    Wattle. Slash w/**wearyall** zedded Heart,

    These drifted Clorn Inx,
          cluttery,
        corn of Cloth –
           freer to gold –

These Tant twisted
      Hood-
         Gleams,
Grieve Stammered Ark Dash Elderns

plummeted
fuselage
Caesura –

**BLACK
DO**
This/

drawn RED –

    wetting out into nitrogen bunching –

**Readiness of
UN-**
    REST,

        BLEED
    browed paw

      pied
     pitchfork –
these skid-eagled ox goads

LICK-KNIVED

DETOUR –

       PLUNDER –

Ferocious Teal –

   HEAD-
     STANDS,

   LOVE-
     SONATAS,

      these –

Provocations,

              these –
         Candle Arias,
              these –

        tenderly,
                 Doves,
                        till

                BONESPIT –

Darned-in-the-cloud –

         Licker Nettles,
            bash boards,
                queasy implements –

These malignant silvers amputated w/out anaesthetic –
These very last bloods –
These stained flowers maimed in the pocket –
These runnered hells on termy wicks –
These wintered sky-cracked astors –
pluming air w/wrecked bending
                BLEED,
                   BLUED-BONE
                   ZIG-ZAG

Chucked Confetti Chaser –
        Calypso
             Corrections –

IT ROVES –

cast-on
stouted
Mortuary-Wrap.
Halts in the Rush –
swinish, extravagant
bereavements –

BRIAR & CLASH

mimicry grids
(PLEURISY GARLANDS)

Parfait witches,
Peat in the Sky –
Viper's Crisp.

It fined stag,
it cowgown,
Punched Blood
powdered Patchouli/
vein of dire
HAWK –
empty intersections –
DASH –
Denied Bitters –
pulling days

These cramped, milter-down, gaulish these jaundiced
days,
these days be
Shudder Couplets,

Chevron
      Suffering/
         Surges/Castle Palettes –
            (Paso Doble) –

               double agents –

Bait & Flood.
Flukes & Clashes.
GORED
     jugular
          buckled –
          deathsea Sapphire –
             SWAN SOB –
           Age within the Leaf
           collisions/
              must/
                 mix-out/
          ate – bumpted, bittered
             burr
                cinder/
                    immense

Cresent Foolery.

            *

Dog Braid.
Wolf's Throth.
Seldomer Cometh,
        Incurved
    Discolorations –
        Deletions – Distortions –

Access & Barriers.
Shouted
Mummeries, Granite

      on the Gut –
    (WHIP WEED, CLOUT)

       copped mortar

Strick Hips
Away –
        denier scaldings –
           Torried honeyed Bisto
              piled hula-bloods,
          Cha-Cha sorried
            scarab
       sullen hiss denominators –
           Morpha Disrupted –

Other Mercies.

A Broad Turken
Dribb Tablish Curer.

(Monkey Tells a Prize/Monkey Gives a Joke).

Be.
That.
As.
It:
May.

Trancers –
Toyed Mead/Can-Can Kiddy
clustering
Bitumen Stutter Clarels.
Hoodlum
Killer-Jewels, Drag-to-Glass
Deadly
thick
SIGHTS OF THE SICK.

*

A LESSON FROM THE COCKEREL

POPPY THANE. PENDLE DUST. BOLDO SACHET GAUDLES
GIVE GINGER. GIVE INK. SMUDGE JEEDELA LEAVINGS,
TWITCH **JULCE.** WORSEN. WRIST DRIP. SKINDA. JANDLE.

UDDER DIADEMS INTERLUCE.
ICYCLE OPALINE RONDA.

CRIMINAL   CRAB RATTLES ON THE LUTE.
CONSTITUENTS   BLINDINGLY RAZOR-GUT.
SHOOKER — GREENEY CRIMSON
NEAPTIDE COMMON PEAKS IN THE
SWIFT PULLERY. TWAIL,
HOYA METHODS: SAXA ANGLAISE

SKEWERED **SKULL** INULA.

2nd LESSON FROM THE COCKEREL

RIVERCRAFT. CAREY NEON. DOVE-WEBBING FATIGUES.
THE SASHED, **SILENT** ONE WHO **HEARS.** THEN AS ONE WHO.
CONJURING SPAT LIGHTS ON THE PALATE. MUSEY TIGHT
SADDED, HAWDY KERDY'S, RAGE RUGGING JET. PORTAGE

RIGHT-HAND
PASSAGEWORK

THICKENS (NEVERINE SPARROWS IN
THE MOUTH BLISTER). RED STROUDERS
DEW-BUCKLING WINTER, TONGUE-A-SAD-
OF-ALL-BIRDS WHEN THE WAVES COME
BONED, BLEED LICKS THE SWIRE-HEAD.
THE DONE-SKIRT. THE SCALDING.
THE SHOT-OVER BELLIES READ WITH
JASPER, MINCE, THE MASSIVE SHIVERS,
LOOF, SWOLE: **JUTTING MULTIPLICATION.**

By Heart –

small fields,
symmetrical tendernesses,
Ox
words, lone

Crouched Burials:

Itinerant Hungers
coining LIVE
BLACK
systems out over mouth –

Skirmishes –
(Astonishingly
Citric) –

.

Alder
ADDER LAID

paysies & marigolds

these bone mace incinerated mauves, lemons
bluedy ails across them/
swaddled,
sulked, salter
spidering clouds of
poisoned fist
& smiley fan –

these Larden Blind Bone Trees –
Bled
in the wound –
cut little blades
of Order/
VOMITED/flighted
on the shelf

severe

unfurling

(hovers

&

shadow)

Dock on the Shoulder – squill vinegar –
LEAP DIRTS
weed moves
in pump
of clenched fist –

Blood
Black
Ruby too took
dark sadly sodden, cuppy
laid inwards
under-Earth/carrion
into
bud clamorous

lachrymal stars
ABRUPTLY
silhouettes –

coaxed. Day,
Beacon as a flight
around mouth –
lowly clover twisted this way,
that way, Pulses
COBALT
in living & in dying –

downed/wooden shatter –

COLD
COLD slumpted Clam-Away
    Tearing
    Circleth –

    Tinner's Arrow –

–   **SKULL**
    Edge,

    frailty,
    Names for Cry –

        thorn in the Arteries –
          sprigged
        Blacks in the ear –
            inched, inhaled
          hidden, these Burners
           boned
        into beaten
            bangings at the
              door.

           *

Kite Acrids, curdled clannish
Affixed
Tidal Broken Bloods in the Sail.

Immaculate Howl –

Extinctions
Abruptly

chains
UPON THE SKULL

Meat Brooch,
dripping
tumult, frantic
folded, quivering
shifted,
suddenly

A Confluence of Robed Spike,
Vestigial,
Nuanced,
Angered.
Warning, Warning, Paper, Paper, Paper, **WARNING**.
Hath Bled Into
Gut-Meter, Few Sheave,
Clan-Get.

Five branches
in one starry street/Lightning w/a
tallow

Sootness.   Para-
STANCE
in each house,
      lie after lie
          after lie

Bombings

& invasion.

Fire, Wipey Pike-A-Peeling,
Antler-Chalice, Jungled Litanies
Iz Lightning
& gadgetry.   Crashed
Mountain Aggregates Kill People
Sick:

      As To
      Scream or So,

the Blandings Midden
dwell narcotic

fold-&-box
the season diminutive, desolate
Bull the Teeth
Strodestink
Sickerbloods,   bargeyful
Captured, Enacted Become, Entangled Die,

Exempting Confections

when the hides are drawn
                in the book
        & the waves are piled
                Black:
        punctured membrane,
                Bill of
        bone & shroud –

Mammal Asinge, Calced Cry a loud lowest food
                ,where the morning is
                raw

        Throat Broken
        Kidsound,
                whipped one eye –
                                sitting fresions –

Ash cherry
        WOKE
        WAY –

        LAID –

        WAY –

Bloody licking,
each solitary view. Colder as the
bright weather comes down
Under Floodlight.   Succinct

Dismemberment.

                        Crier Came

Dead.

OTHER TITLES FROM REALITY STREET EDITIONS, 1993-2006

Poetry series
1993
Kelvin Corcoran: *Lyric Lyric*, £5.99
Susan Gevirtz: *Taken Place*, £6.50
Maggie O'Sullivan: *In the House of the Shaman*, £6.50
Denise Riley: *Mop Mop Georgette*, £6.50
1994
Allen Fisher: *Dispossession and Cure*, £6.50
1995
Fanny Howe: *O'Clock*, £6.50
Sarah Kirsch: *T* (O/P)
Peter Riley: *Distant Points* (O/P)
1996
Maggie O'Sullivan (ed.): *Out of Everywhere*, £12.50
1997
Nicole Brossard: *Typhon Dru*, £5.50
Cris Cheek/Sianed Jones: *Songs From Navigation* (+ audio CD), £12.50
Lisa Robertson: *Debbie: an Epic*, £7.50*
Maurice Scully: *Steps*, £6.50
1998
Barbara Guest: *If So, Tell Me* (O/P)
2000
Tony Lopez: *Data Shadow*, £6.50
Denise Riley: *Selected Poems*, £7.50
2001
Anselm Hollo (ed. & tr.): *Five From Finland*, £7.50
Lisa Robertson: *The Weather*, £7.50*
2003
Ken Edwards: *eight + six*, £7.50
Robert Sheppard: *The Lores*, £7.50
Lawrence Upton: *Wire Sculptures*, £5
2004
David Miller: *Spiritual Letters (I-II)*, £6.50
Redell Olsen: *Secure Portable Space*, £7.50
Peter Riley: *Excavations*, £9
2005
Allen Fisher: *Place*, £15
Tony Baker: *In Transit*, £7.50
2006
Jeff Hilson: *stretchers*, £7.50
Maurice Scully: *Sonata*, £8.50

* co-published with New Star Books, Vancouver, BC

4Packs series
1996
1: *Sleight of Foot* (Miles Champion, Helen Kidd, Harriet Tarlo, Scott Thurston)
1998
2: *Vital Movement* (Andy Brown, Jennifer Chalmers, Mike Higgins, Ira Lightman)
1999
3: *New Tonal Language* (Patricia Farrell, Shelby Matthews, Simon Perril, Keston Sutherland)
2002
4: *Renga+* (Guy Barker, Elizabeth James/Peter Manson, Christine Kennedy)

Narrative series
1998
Ken Edwards: *Futures*
2005
John Hall: *Apricot Pages*
David Miller: *The Dorothy and Benno Stories*
Douglas Oliver: *Whisper 'Louise'*

Go to www.realitystreet.co.uk, email info@realitystreet.co.uk or write to the address on the reverse of the title page for updates.

Become a Reality Street Supporter!

Since 1998, more than 70 individuals and organisations have helped Reality Street Editions by being Reality Street Supporters. Those signed up to the Supporter scheme from 2003-2006 are listed below .

The Supporter scheme is an important way to keep Reality Street's programme of adventurous writing alive. When you sign up as a Supporter for a year, you receive all titles published in that year, and your name printed in the back of the books, as below (unless you prefer anonymity). For more information, go to www.realitystreet.co.uk or email info@realitystreet.co.uk

Peter Barry
Charles Bernstein
Clive Bush
Richard Cacchione
CCCP
Adrian Clarke
Mark Dickinson
Michael Finnissy
Allen Fisher/Spanner
Sarah Gall
Chris Goode
John Hall
Alan Halsey
Robert Hampson
Peter Hodgkiss
Fanny Howe
Harry Gilonis &
    Elizabeth James
Lisa Kiew
Peter Larkin
Tony Lopez
Ian McMillan
Richard Makin
Jules Mann
Mark Mendoza

Peter Middleton
Geraldine Monk
Maggie O'Sullivan
Marjorie Perloff
Pete & Lyn
Peter Philpott
Tom Quale
Peter Quartermain
Ian Robinson
Will Rowe
Susan Schultz
Maurice Scully
Robert Sheppard
John Shreffler
Peterjon & Yasmin Skelt
Hazel Smith
Valerie & Geoffrey Soar
Tony Trehy
Keith Tuma
Sam Ward
John Welch/The Many Press
John Wilkinson
Tim Woods
The Word Hoard
+ 8 anonymous